Watch My Back
The Geoff Thompson Story

Part One

Geoff Thompson

SUMMERSDALE

Summersdale Publishers Ltd
46 West Street
Chichester
PO19 1RP
United Kingdom

A CIP catalogue record for this book is available from the British Library.

Printed and bound in Great Britain by Caledonian International Book Manufacturing Ltd, Glasgow.

ISBN 1 84024 080 6

Photographs by David W Monks
Member of the Master Photographer's Association
Snappy Snaps Portrait Studio
7 Cross Cheaping
Coventry
CV1 1HF

About the author

Geoff Thompson has to be one of the most recognised and controversial martial arts writers and teachers of this century, with over 20 bestselling books and 20 instructional videos on the contemporary role of martial art to his name. His work is both innovative and thought-provoking. As an ambassador for the martial arts he has appeared on national and international television and radio – for several years as the *BBC Good Morning* self-defence expert – talking about and giving advice on self-protection and related subjects.

He has taught his unique method of self-protection to the police, the marines, in local government, on Excel Bodyguard training camps and also on the professional circuit. He has appeared in numerous publications including: *SG's Martial Arts*, *Combat*, *Traditional Karate*, *Fighters*, *Terry O'Neill's Fighting Arts International*, *Muscle Mag* (Britain – USA), *Black Belt Magazine* (USA) *Fighters* (Sweden) and *Australasian Fighting Arts* (Australia). He is currently Sub-Editor of *Martial Arts Illustrated*. He has also featured in mainstream glossy magazines such as *Loaded*, *Maxim* and *Esquire* and has published several articles with *GQ* Magazine (Britain – Paris).

Geoff has to be one of the most practised instructors of our day with a long list of combat qualifications. He is presently a Sambo Russian Wrestling coach (Moscow Sambo Federation), Olympic Greco Roman Wrestling Coach (FILA), Olympic Free Style Level 3 Wrestling Coach (FILA) Ju-Jitsu coach, British Combat Association Coach, EKGB (Karate) 5th Dan, JKA (Japan Karate Association) 2nd Dan, Shoalin Modga gung fu 1st Dan, BJA (British Judo Association) 1st Dan, ABA boxing coach and BTBC Muay Thai boxing coach. He is a former UK weapons champion and is trained in the use of the Defensive Flashlight and the PR24 Side Handled Baton. He has also trained in Aikido and weapons.

In 1997 Geoff was flown out to the United States by Chuck Norris and Richard Norton to teach his unique method of self-protection on their international martial arts seminar alongside martial art greats: Benny 'the jet' Urquediz and Rigan and Jean-Jacques Machado.

As well as his books and videos Geoff has written a feature film based on his life and 12 television plays based on his bouncer books. Although recognised as an international authority on the art of self-protection, his work in reality and cross training in combat is still thought of as heresy in some quarters of the martial arts world.

Acknowledgements

Thanks to John 'Awesome' Anderson for being a great teacher and friend.

Thanks to Stewart and Alastair of Summersdale for commissioning *Watch My Back* and starting me on the literary path.

To Mum and Dad, I love you.

To Sharon, my life, my inspiration.

Also

to Kerry, Lisa, Jennie and Louis,

my beautiful, beautiful children,

and

to my late, great friend, Mick Brennan.

Always show respect, so when
evil rears its ugly head
You'll be justified to then
show the iron hand instead.

Seek to be humble,
Humility is the mark of greatness.

Coventry

The three spired city
That inspired pity
On the cap with the button
The Industrious glutton.

Ray Thompson.

Contents

Introduction   8

Prologue   9

1. Early days. From little acorns oak trees grow   12

2. A change in direction   20

3. The good   23

4. The bad and the ugly   32

5. Fighting without fighting   50

6. Police involvement   57

7. Come-ons and come-backs   73

8. Street fighters and trained fighters   92

9. Man-made misconceptions   111

10. David and Goliath   127

11. Humour in adversity   136

12. Dealing with women   143

13. The hunters and the hunted   153

Epilogue   172

Introduction

Watch My Back is not simply a book about violence and not a book about Martial Arts, although it is written by a successful Martial Artist and a man who has made violence his profession. Rather it is a book about coping with fear in an environment which is a culture dish for modern society - today's nightclubs.

The seemingly mindless violence that certain individuals are prepared to inflict on others is not restricted to only nightly venues in Coventry, but can now be found daily on our streets and even the average man from those streets will find something in this book which may at some time prove life saving. Not 'quick fix' physical techniques, but attitude, which in certain circumstances may be all that will see him through.

For Martial Artists this book will be a bitter but honest pill to swallow. What they follow as an art is seldom practical when needed and it may be safer for them to face that fact and their fears from the safety of these covers than to put themselves in the situations faced by its author.

A true tale of modern violence and its containment lightened by the very necessary vein of humour never far below the surface of every chapter.

Peter Consterdine, 7th Dan
Joint Chief Instructor British Combat Association

Prologue

The saddest truth you will ever hear is that violence can only be stopped by greater violence, whether it is on the school playground where the bully dishes out misery on those weaker than himself or on the bloodied battlefields of war.

Politicians and Law Lords will, and have, denied this truth emphatically, because to admit it is to invite it in, as I can well understand. While they deny it orally they do not in deed. What happened when Hitler decided he was going to take the world by force for his own domination and rule and no amount of talks or negotiations were about to stop him? What did the British government do when Argentina would not, when asked, pull out of the Falkland Islands that they had taken by force? And what did the United Nations consider 'justifiable action' when Saddam Hussein would not listen to reason? WAR!! The greatest expression of violence known to man. Violence is very wrong, but sometimes it is necessary in the interests of peace.

Without violence in my life, let me tell you, my world would be a better and happier place. But, alas, the way the world is going I fear my dreams will never be realised.

My own personal perception of a doorman is a person who welcomes people to an establishment, protects the good majority from the bad minority and the indifferent from themselves whilst on the premises and bids them good night at the end of the evening. The bullying, sadistic type of doorman so often portrayed by the media is in my mind a minority. The 'job' is similar to that of a policeman: thankless, and though very much needed in today's society it is, sadly, greatly misunderstood.

So, I would be very grateful if, when you read this book, you would do so with an open mind. Try to rid yourself of any pre-conceived misconceptions you may have about doormen, and please try to be brutally honest with yourself, perhaps putting yourself in my position when evaluating my character. If you only skim the surface of this book you may only see a fighter. If you are looking for a man of violence then that is, also, all you will find. If, however, you are perceptive enough to look deeper, then hopefully you will see the real me: a kind, sensitive, soft man who threw himself into the volcano of life in a desperate bid to learn how to handle the heat, a man who was being bullied and pushed around by life and was so sick and in pain with his own weaknesses that the fear of confronting life seemed lesser than carrying on living life as a worm. So if, in your estimation, I have portrayed myself as being a little over-zealous in my bid to better myself then please forgive me — it was the only way I knew how.

'Working the door' to me was a means to an end. I could ill afford to go to Japan, the Mecca of Martial Arts, like many before me to build my spirit and character, but my experiences 'on the door' meant that I didn't have to. I only had to go as far as myself. By confronting my fears and facing my demons I began my long walk down the road to mind mastery.

There is more than one path to the peak of the mountain. 'Bouncing' has taught me to live a braver life; my spirit and mind are ever strengthening. I have also developed my own theory on fear control, and although complete mastery is still a long way off, I have at least found my own personal way. Born to these strengths are, I'm afraid to say, slight paranoia and contempt for disrespectful people, though I have developed a will strong enough to, in time, slay both.

Karate, first and foremost, teaches humility and respect. If more people were humble and showed a little more respect to their fellow human beings there would be no need for doormen and we'd be living in a world without wars. What a lovely thought...

Watch My Back to me half a year to write down and another year to finish. The first six months' worth was penned whilst sitting on the loo in the engineering factory that employed me, hiding from the unsuspecting, tyrannical foreman who loved to hate me. Needless to say I no longer work there, otherwise my words would not be so brave or revealing. Six months sitting on the toilet, though, is not to be recommended. I now suffer loss of feeling in my legs and a permanent red ring around my bum.

The book tells of my experiences working as a bouncer over the last eight years in the suburbs and city centre of Coventry, once polled as the most violent city for its size and population in Europe. As a claim to fame, I feel it leaves the city short changed. But what do I know? I've only lived there all my life.

As I am not prone to exaggeration you can rely on this text to be an honest and truthful account of the occurrences that have made me laugh and cry, and have left me shocked, disturbed, impressed and at times downright amazed. I will tell of friends, enemies, pimps, prostitutes, cowards and heroes. I hope you enjoy it in the reading as much as I did in the writing. Please believe me when I say I do not write to shock, only to educate. If I have a weakness I will admit it; my strength I will also show. But for my literary honesty please do not brand me a coward or a braggart.

Chapter 1

Early days.
From little acorns oak trees grow

Before I recount my experiences, I think it is best that I tell you a little of my early days so that you may appreciate that any ability or strength I have now was bitterly fought for, and, though I say so myself, well earned. Also, hopefully it will enlighten you as to why a man such as myself entered the many splendoured world of a doorman.

All my early life, certainly from the age of eleven, I was plagued by the fear of fighting and confrontations. My mind was weak and constantly under attack from fears too powerful to defend against. Doubtless I was not on my own in this respect, but at the time I felt I was, so I could take no solace in the former. What I found to my distaste was not 'being scared' but the thought of having to live under its dominion for the rest of my life.

Many's the time I found myself sneaking out of the school's back entrance to avoid my would-be antagonists waiting for me at the front, and running off to the sanctuary of short-sightedness and ignorance only to wake up the next morning with fear and worry ever-growing at the thought of having to go back to school and face the 'enemy' again, often having to go under the protective wing of my Dad.

I vividly remember one Christmas morning sitting in my bedroom alone and crying, worrying about going back to school in two weeks' time, and the misery that would then ensue, and my elder brother coming in and asking me what was wrong. I shrugged my shoulders, too ashamed to admit my weakness. My whole childhood was marred by such incidents: these sad, scared, worried feelings came and went at will - I was at the mercy of my own mind.

Hope came on the horizon in the guise of the Martial Arts. Bruce Lee took on all 'celluloid' comers and held no fear. He became my mentor and I enthusiastically, though not convincingly, mimicked him along with thousands of other proteges of the late great. This was my first and biggest misconception in the Martial Arts, to believe the drivel of celluloid Martial Arts. It took ten long years of experimenting and soul searching before I could finally admit to myself that 'real fighting' wasn't like that. Anyway I plodded on, conscientiously learning technique if nothing else. Confidence was born to better technique and by my fourth year in comprehensive school I had begun to feel less scared, the bullies of yesteryear were confronted and beaten and tossed by the wayside. My fears were temporarily checked, only to be replaced by a weakness as great in its own right, overconfidence. I had reached an embryonic peak and mistook overconfidence for fearlessness.

I had worked and trained hard and believed my lack of fear to be the fruit of my labour. I realised later, much later, that the goal was not to rid myself of fear (that can never happen), more to control and harness it. Anyway, there I was, sixteen, left Aikido and by now a purple belt in Shotokan Karate, standing on a 'sugar pedestal', not realising that when the rain came down it would crumble below.

Inevitably, the rain did come, in the shape of a six foot, thirteen stone (or at least he seemed that big) Jamaican called Ronnie. He had a face like a robber's dog and a growl to match. His hands were the biggest things I'd ever seen without lungs and he wanted me. I'd given his mate 'tarmac burns' the week before, and done it with little or no fear, and Ron was not H.P. when he approached me to tell me so. I felt the explosion inside, my legs shook and seemed to cry out 'overload, overload'. That little man popped up on my shoulder and said, 'Now you're fucked, ain't ya?'

In retrospect he was probably as wary of me as I was of him, but he hid it well and I didn't. The arse dropped out of my trousers and the sugar pedestal crumbled below me, leaving me back on the unfriendly floor of reality. Fear and worry were back on the curriculum. Insecurity crept back in, and every time I felt even a little confident I subconsciously reminded myself of 'Ronnie the robber's dog'. I still kept up the Shotokan but found it hard in a tough club under the auspices of sensei Rick Jackson. I was 'catching a few' and didn't like it, thank you very much. The fear that had dissipated returned with a vengeance. Just getting to the dojo became a battle, and an hour and a half's training seemed more like a week and a half. I'd look up at the clock and it would say 7.30, I'd look again in an hour's time and it'd only be 7.35.

Time distortion seemed to have it in for me, and being hit was not exactly fun. Now that I understand training I realise that if you're not getting hit, or if there isn't at least the danger of it, it becomes unrealistic and impractical as a form of self-defence. 'If you want to dance to the music, you have to pay the band'. Every time I used to go training I'd pop my head through the high wooden dojo door to see who was there. If I saw anyone who was likely to 'give it to me', my heart would sink to my stomach, and fear, worry and time distortion ganged up on me like a pack of wolves. This kind of pressure coupled with the discovery of my 'mating tackle' forced me to into early retirement from Karate, and for the time being I was content to live with the fears and misconceptions.

I married young, and had our first child at eighteen years of age. Things looked different now, I had a wife and a child to protect. If I wasn't capable of doing that, what good was I? With this thought acting as my sponsor and catalyst, I began training again, this time with sifu Alan Hines in Shaolin Motga Gung Fu, a form of Chinese boxing. I restarted my search. I eventually attained my black-belt in Gung Fu, but after some disagreements with my sempais (not Alan) I decided to leave and go back to shotokan. I trained very hard, but there were many times when I felt like throwing it all in. Even when I gained my black belt in Shotokan I still didn't feel mentally stronger.

I'd reached the physical goals I had set myself, and hoped along the way my 'mental physique' would develop and I would erase my fear of 'real fighting'. At times I kidded myself that I had, but I hadn't. I still worried that I couldn't control the massive explosion

I felt inside every time I even smelt trouble. There was one occasion when I did rise above my fears.

My Dad was brushing close to fifty five, and you couldn't meet a more amicable, placid chap. I love him. The two half-wits who followed him out of the working men's club one late weekend evening never, unfortunately, shared my love. My sister, sixteen at the time, her girlfriend and their two equally juvenile boyfriends walked from the club slightly ahead of my Mum and Dad. The chat was light and cheerful as they walked down the pavement towards home. The two that followed them were of ill intent. One was tall and weasel-faced, with heavily tattooed arms, the other was short and stocky with short hair, a pig's nose and narrow, mean eyes. Both were in their late 'teens. My family had no knowledge of their presence until they struck, in a completely unprovoked, mindless assault.

They set about the two young boys arm in arm with my sister and her friend, beating them mercilessly to the ground. The young girls screamed in horror and begged for the slaughter to stop, but their pleas met only the vulgarity of verbal abuse. My Dad, being of the old school, ran in to separate hunter and its prey, expecting a little respect due to his seniority, but got a hefty blow to the eye that sent him crashing to the floor. He then received several heavy kicks to his face and body, and watched, semi-conscious, as the two kicked the still-horizontal youths so hard that their jelly, lifeless bodies shifted along the floor. Dad's face twisted in a writhing mask of pain.

This wasn't the first time they had done this; mine wasn't the first father to meet with their wrath. They were, by all accounts, making a bit of a career of violence, and were meeting little or no resistance. Their names were big in a wide spectrum of the area, and because of this they were suffering no comebacks for their unsolicited onslaughts.

This time, though, they'd made a mistake. This time it was my Dad they'd done.

Courtaulds was a big, thriving chemical plant in the north of the city and could be smelt for miles around. Its musty, vinegary, property-devaluing fragrance dug deep into its workers' paws and infested itself into their clothes, cars and furniture. Everything, in fact, with which it came into contact. I hated working there.

No one had told me of Dad's attack. The first I knew of it was when I saw its aftermath in the form of the lumps and black bruises that covered his face as we met by the works canteen. My greeting smile dissipated instantly and my stammering mouth searched for words but found none. My eyes welled with a blurry, salty film and my anger grew. I prayed that his injuries were just the result of an unfortunate, silly accident, but I knew my prayers lay on thin ice.

My Dad unfolded the pages of his encounter. As the details scratched into my heart and etched themselves onto the plateau of my mind I silently swore my revenge. Dad wanted an end to it, Mum warned me to 'leave it', but the hurt inside me wouldn't let it lie. I had to let them, Dad's attackers, and everyone else for that matter, know that you don't mess with my kin and get away with it.

A month of detective work, asking anyone and everyone about the incident, resulted in the names Grinsell and Davis. By the time my search had ended I had addresses and telephone numbers. I knew more about them than their own mothers. I also knew that their time was running out. I decided not to phone them or visit their homes because they both had families and I didn't want to involve innocent parties. I would just bide my time and wait for the right moment.

The door knocker of my third floor maisonette echoed at the 10.45 pm knock. I opened the door to reveal Ken, my wife's brother.

'They're at the club now, Geoff.'

His simple message filled me with a concoction of fear and excitement. This was what I had been waiting for: my time and their time had come. I bowed the laces of my polished black, steel toe-capped 'equalisers' and made my way to the club.

The huge, high-ceilinged concert room in the newly-built working men's club was filled to capacity. My eyes searched through old and young, tall and short, for the pair. Ken pointed

Grinsell out to me as he headed for the toilet in the corner of the room. My blood raced and I smiled to myself as I thought of doing the dirty deed in the loo, forcing his head into the urinal. But attractive as the idea seemed, it wasn't practical - too many witnesses and too many people to stop me. I didn't want to be stopped.

'I know what you're doing here,' said Steve, a tall, ginger-haired friend of mine, interrupting my thoughts. 'He's bad news, Geoff, be careful. He always carries a knife. I know you do Karate Geoff, but be careful,' he added, shaking his head.

I knew he was concerned, but I also knew he was trying to worry-monger me and I felt a little insulted that he thought I would be put off so easily. Didn't he know that this was blood?

The last fifteen minutes of the night had me waiting in slow motion. I watched as Grinsell and Davis left their seats on the low balcony that rose slightly above and back from the sunken dance floor, two young girls following them as they passed Ken and I on their exit, not catching the look of hate I threw from my despising eyes. We followed them out onto the pavement, appropriately only a yard from where they'd done my Dad. Their laughing and joking ceased as I approached them from the rear.

'Hey, mate!' I called, with a slight quiver in my voice. Grinsell turned his head to me. I hated him, despised him, loathed him, I wanted and needed to hurt him. Everything I despised in a person was epitomised in this piece of shit that stood before me, that dared to share the same pavement as myself, that had the audacity to breathe the same air. I saw my Dad's face stretching in pain, felt his anguish as boot after boot landed heavily on his face, and sensed his feeling of absolute helplessness at the hands of this scum.

'BANG!' I put my right steel toe-capped foot into his eye, busting it into a gaping, bleeding wound, the contact of steel on bone sounding like a hammer hitting a girder. He landed heavily on the grass verge behind him, the two lady companions jumped back in fright. Davis took a stance in front of me, his hands circling in a celluloid Kung-Fu style, puffing and sucking air in and out, trying, badly, to control his fear.

I took his measure then ploughed a left leg roundhouse into his lower abdomen. He crumpled over like a folded penknife, though before I could finish the job Ken, who was only light-framed and young, lashed into him with fists and feet, leaving him blood scarlet. Grinsell, who had obviously never played major league before, recovered some of his senses and ran for it. I gave chase, hurling much abuse at his yellow back. Two hundred yards up the road, when I thought I'd almost lost the chase, he tripped and fell: all my Christmases and birthdays came at once as I vented the anger that had been bubbling inside me. He covered up his head and crouched up his body as I kicked his frame savagely from head to foot. He begged me to stop but I couldn't. I kept seeing my Dad's battered face in my mind.

My body, which had been aching for revenge, went into overdrive and only his whimpering, begging pleas for mercy eventually stopped me. Was this weak specimen at my feet really the tough guy I'd been warned to be careful of? Was he really the man I ought not to have crossed? He was nothing and will always be nothing. Sometimes now, ten years on, I still see Grinsell and he cowers under my shadow.

As the skin tightened around the birth and abundance of his bulging bruises, I celebrated the death of his reign, as did his many other victims.

Through my searching and experimenting I learned that the explosion inside my stomach that I had struggled so much to control was the adrenalin build-up, the 'fight or flight' syndrome, a chemical release from the adrenal gland that hits and goes through the blood stream like a speeding tube train, preparing the body to fight or flight. It makes you temporarily stronger and faster, and partially anaesthetises you from pain. The more dangerous the situation, the bigger the build-up and adrenalin release; the bigger the release the better you perform. But by the same count the bigger the build-up and release the harder it is to control, ie. the easier it is for you to bottle out.

Cus Damatio once said that the feeling of fear is as natural as the feeling of hunger or thirst or of wanting to use the toilet. When you're hungry you eat, when you're thirsty you drink, and so it should be with the feeling of fear: you shouldn't panic under it, you should harness and then utilise it. So my goal became to control and master fear, rather than to erase it.

Now came the hard part, putting theory into practise. I needed exposure to stressful situations in a bid to conjure up fear in the hope that in confronting that fear I would become desensitised to it. 'Confrontation Desensitisation', if you like. How to go about it though? I couldn't just go out and look for trouble - that would be going against the strict moral and ethical codes of Karate, and also the law of Karma, 'A good for a good, and a bad for a bad'.

The only way I could find around this was 'bouncing' in the Coventry pubs and night spots. But I had to ask myself if I could hack it: Coventry seemed more famous these days for the monopoly it held on violence than for its three spires and cathedral. I was riddled with self-doubt. What if I got hammered? What if my bottle went? Getting the job wouldn't be too much of a problem with a black belt in Karate, but if I was a success and held the position any length of time I knew the bow tie on white shirt would effectively mean I had to take on all-comers. I was having a severe attack of the 'Jonah complex', or in laymen's terms a fear of success. Abraham Moslow, the famous humanist psychologist, stated,

'We are generally afraid to become that which we can glimpse in our most perfect moments, under the most perfect conditions, under conditions of greatest courage, we enjoy and even thrill to the God-like possibilities we see in ourselves at such peak moments, and yet, simultaneously, we shiver with weakness, awe and fear before the same possibilities.' So if I did raise the moral fibre to propel me into the kitchen of violence, could I stand the heat once there? The thought of living with my fears seemed to me to be worse than the fear of getting beaten up, in that the former was long-term, ie. forever, and the latter was short-term. So began my term of office 'on the door'.

Chapter 2

A change in direction

Initially, no matter how hard I tried, and believe me I did try hard, I just could not make the techniques that I had learnt over the past few years work for me in a live situation. Yet all around me were people who hadn't a day's formal training to their name, controlling and winning every situation that challenged them - and without breaking into a sweat.

At first I found it very confusing, but after much analysis and soul searching I came to the conclusion that the knowledge I was carrying could and would work for me, but it needed a little adjusting. This was something of a dilemma. Of course I could add and subtract from the syllabus whatever I wanted, but was it ethical to butcher an art that had been developed over hundreds of years by many Masters, just to suit my own needs? Perhaps the weakness was not in the art itself but in me. Maybe I was just not good enough to work the system. Maybe I was even demeaning the art that I loved by working on the door in the first place. What right did I have to blow against the wind? These were just a few of the problems my mind was wrestling with.

Hypothetically, just suppose I packed in the door for moral or whatever reasons and a situation arose whereby I had to defend myself. Where would I be knowing that the art would not work effectively for me in its present form, and I refused to change it? Lying half dead in a road side gutter where the darker side of society had left me? My final conclusion was that change was necessary for survival.

I was and always have been primarily a kicker, but this had to change. So I joined a boxing club. I had little or no knowledge of grappling, so I started to learn judo. I also changed my attitude to training. To all you kickers out there, keep kicking but please learn to punch. I am not against kicking but it's simply a matter of logic. Most violent situations can be attributed to drink, and occur in pubs, clubs etc. In such places there simply isn't any kicking room. Next time you are in a pub or club, look around you. You'd be lucky to find room to throw a punch, let alone a kick. The situations where you do have the luxury of kicking distance are few and far between, and that distance can be lost quicker than virginity in Hillfields. Kicking also expends twice the energy of punching, and because you are using your legs to kick you have lost some of your mobility. On the plus side, they are second to none if you are in the privileged position of having your opponent on the ground. There is no better tool for finishing off than the feet. There is also a definite need for close range punches such as hooks and uppercuts. Grappling is also essential if you lose punching range, as often happens. Probably 70% of fights end up in grappling range.

Attitude! This was where my biggest change was made. All the fighting ability in the world won't help if you haven't got the moral fibre to use it. Some people will tell you that if you weren't born with bottle you'll never get it. If I thought that was true I would never teach Karate again. When God gave out bottle I think I must have been at the back of the queue, but I figured if I could confront all my fears I would have no fears, and logically would have loads of bottle.

This I did, and it made me much stronger-minded. However, that feeling of fear, I soon discovered, would never go away. It was, in fact, a force of strength. It can help you when you are hindered, keep you on your feet when you feel like dropping, send you victorious against outstanding odds and warm your whole body against the cold of the world. Let it off the leash and it will dominate and rule you, hurt you and maybe even kill you.

Cus Damatio once said, 'Fear is the friend of exceptional people'. How could I become an exceptional person and make fear my friend? That was the question. The only way to get used to the feeling was to experience it, not to read about it or talk about it or imagine it. The first and most important thing I did, of course, was to start working on the door.

The next thing was to change the way I actually trained; not so much the content but the way I actually practised them. If I was kicking, punching, blocking etc. in the air I no longer performed the techniques just for the sake of it - I threw them with intent and used visualisation. I imagined an assailant in front of me, and imagined the effect that the technique would have on him and perhaps how I would feel if the situation were real.

When it came to partner work, he/she was an enemy and when I attacked I never attacked to miss like so many people do, I attacked to hit, every single time. This would often get my opponent's back up, so when it came to their turn to attack they would really try to get me. All of a sudden the set partner work was no longer a game.

Chapter 3

The good

The name 'bouncer' has always been, or so it would seem, synonymous with violence. Violence does play a predominant role at times, but it's there out of necessity rather than desire. Most doormen I have worked with have been good doormen. The bad ones, the egoistic, bullying types are only partly to blame for the bad reputation we seem to carry. The blame in fact mostly lies with the general run of the mill punter whose ignorance in doorman and doorwork seems larger than an elephant's condom. More often than not they witness an altercation in its culminating stages - generally a doorman hitting or ejecting someone - and then draw a conclusion on the basis of the tiny percentage of the altercation that they have seen. 'The bouncer hit that man for absolutely no reason' is a typical comment, or 'there was no need for that, it was over the top' is another. No doubt there are probably doormen out there who hit out for little or no reason, but they form a minority whom I've yet to come across.

I particularly remember one incident whilst I was working in the Wyken Pippin. I bumped into a chap in the pool room and immediately apologised to him for my clumsiness. For my courtesy he told me in no uncertain terms that if I bumped into him again he was going to push a glass in my face. Dumbfounded, I asked him to repeat what he had said, as I found it difficult to believe. This he did, putting said glass close to my face to reinforce his meaning. So I obliterated him. In five seconds he was all over the carpet. All that the many locals present that night really caught of the situation was me administering myself onto this 'innocent' person. Someone approached me later in the evening and informed me that the locals thought I was out of order.

'Why do you think I hit him?' I asked, more than a little annoyed.

He looked puzzled. He hadn't thought of that.

'Well, I don't really know. Er, why did you hit him?' he asked. 'Don't you think you should have found that out before you condemned me? How long have you known me? Do you really think I would hit someone for no reason? You insult me.'

I then told him in graphic detail 'why' and 'what for'. When I had finished he was very apologetic, but I couldn't help thinking this was probably how many of the 'bad doormen' reputations were built.

I have also had occasions when I've had to 'deal' with people who have attacked, challenged or barracked me, and then watched helplessly while they tell their friends or by-standers that I hit them for absolutely no reason.

One hod carrier turned up for work with two lovely black eyes and told his work mates,

'Geoff Thompson done it. I was just standing there minding my own business when he walked over and punched me right on the nose.'

One of the bricklayers on the site came to my defence,

'I know Geoff and if he's hit you then you needed hitting.'

But to how many other people had he told the same sorry tale where there was nobody to defend my integrity? In some circles my name is probably as black as coal. And that is why trying to convince some people that all doormen are not bad is like trying to tell a white mouse that a black cat is lucky. So I've named this chapter 'The Good' after the doormen, because in my opinion the phrase describes the majority of them.

The fighting and the violence has been severe at times, but, may God forgive me for saying this, sometimes hurting people is/was the only way. If you try to counter violence orally, you will for your pains be bullied, intimidated and eventually become history. As the tale tells and the violence spews out onto the pages of this text, I will try to explain and justify the actions of myself and others.

The first couple of 'doors' I worked were quiet and without incident, and I'm glad because I was 'green' - so green in fact that the other lads nicknamed me Robin Hood. But I was keen: my quick learning was sporned from conscientiousness, hunger and need. The gravity of the job never really hit me until I stepped up a league, leaving pub work for nightclub work. For four years, G's nightclub was unrelentingly rough. If you had more than two teeth they called you a cissy, and the few teeth that the locals did have they dental flossed with a Katana. Everybody coming in to G's was checked for weapons: if they had none they were refused entry for their own safety.

I was thrown in at the deep end, Saturday night sharks and all. It was an eventful night. A huge black guy, who had a face like ten boxers and facial 'mars bars' that made spaghetti junction seem uncomplicated, pulled a knife on me at the entrance to the club, and I had a fight with a chap who took exception to being asked to leave. My adrenalin was on red alert all night.

I remember thinking, 'what the fuck am I doing here? This is a mistake.' There and then I decided that door work wasn't, isn't and never would be for me. This was to be my first and last night. At the end of the night we all sat down in the now empty club for a stiff drink, while the lads laughed and joked about my unfortunate first night. A few compliments about my performance were thrown my way and I guess I got a little high on it. 'Ah, it's not that bad really,' I thought, proud of myself for sticking it a whole night. 'I might as well stay for a bit longer.' This was my introduction to the nightclub scene.

Before long, I got to know the other lads, six in all, really well and felt honoured at being accepted on a door that was without a doubt the strongest and most feared in the city. John was the head doorman and he and I hit it off straight away. He was a veteran doorman, so took me under his war-torn wing. My apprenticeship began and it was to prove a complex one; so many things to do, to learn, to understand. Every single situation that faces you demands a different solution and just when you think you're mastering it all, something would pop up and mock you,

'Ha, never had this happened to you before have you?'

I was happy in the beginning to stand back and watch John. After every incident or fight that I was involved in, John would pull me to one side and tell me where I went right and where I went wrong. This system worked well because John was an able teacher and I a willing student, sponging up the vast knowledge here on tap. He was the first person I had met who seemed to hold the answers to all my questions. He would warn me of all the dangers, hurdles and pitfalls and how I was going to feel before, during and after a fight. All the time we worked together I watched, studied and mimicked him, picking his brains until every thing he knew I knew. This close contact between us gave birth to a camaraderie that would last a lifetime - we became brothers. The irony of it all was that I had spent half of my life training in different fighting arts and there I was, learning and relearning from a man who hadn't done a formal day's fighting training in his life. Being the excellent street fighter and master doorman he was, I pushed my black belt and ego to one side and learnt.

John wasn't big at five foot eight, but carried fourteen stone of superbly cast muscle that set him apart from other men, though his doorman attire curtained his herculean dimensions into the shadow of modesty. A thin, Clark Gable 'tash' lay on caramel skin, above a mouth that mirrored a permanent state of frown, making the occasional smile for only close friends and his short Afro hair was always meticulously neat, as was his black suit with spit polished shining shoes and 'Persil' white shirt. John was laid back and cooler than a December stream, never missed anything and contemplated all. His vicious, brutal temper had been carefully controlled, harnessed and fine-tuned to a laser line of ferocious aggression that could be turned on and off with pin-point accuracy, usually missiled through the medium of a left hook. He also made the duck syndrome his own, although his frowning hard look was often enough to put off most would-be fighters without throwing a punch.

One particular night we'd thrown a couple of lads out of G's for fighting and in the process one of the lads had all the buttons of his shirt ripped off. The young man, steeped in stupidity, decided that he was going to get reimbursed for his loss and turned to John who was closest to him,

'Look at my shirt man, fifty pence a button!'

He aggressively thrust his hand out to John for the money. John remained expressionless, lifted his lighted cigarette to his lips and drew heavily on it, squinting his eyes in thought, then chimneyed the smoke into the astounded face of 'Buttons.'

'How much?' he replied quietly.

'Buttons,' whose face turned from hard to lard, realised he was standing in quick sand and was about to be sucked under. He attempted to pull himself free,

'Twenty pence.' he said almost apologetically.

John shook his head and asked,

'How much do you like your face?'

'A lot,' came the whimpering reply.

'Well you'd better fuck off then,' said John, still in a low tone. No aggression, no violence, job done.

Raf was a friend of a good friend and was now also a good friend. A professional middle weight boxer whose boyish smiling face might, to the uninitiated, suggest that he couldn't box eggs, but the man could 'motor'. At five feet eleven, he was tall for a middle weight and seemed eternally bouncy and bubbly, with always a nice word for everyone. Raf was to humility what Nureyev is to ballet - but what a doorman.

His first door was a rough door, and to all intents and purposes he must have looked out of place with his neat bow tie, friendly gait and sheepish smile in an edge of town 'Bikers' pub which boasted more steel than Sheffield. It was a corner pub with the lounge entrance coming off the main road and the bar entrance off the side road. Directly opposite the bar entrance and across the side road was a small bistro, a magic shop and around the corner, the Odeon cinema. Opposite the lounge entrance and across the main road was the student-infested Coventry Poly.

The bar that Raf was guarding was long and cluttered with 'pantry' chairs and tables that screeched the stone tiled floor like nails on a black board with every movement, even audible above the cafuffle of ten score voices that conversed competitively across every table top where leather sloganed jackets and greasy long hair were the order of the day. A 'suit' entering the bar would render the place completely silent and cast a million disapproving stares. One of the bikers, a pea pod double for Alice Cooper, brave with beer and completely mentally disarmed by this slight amiable doorman fellow, thought he might test the waters. Oily, dirty and piss smelling, he smiled a knowing smile at Raf and nodded his head sardonically,

'What the fuck are you doing on the door?' he asked, threateningly.

Raf looked past him, but monitored his every move.

'I'm paid to do it and I can,' he replied.

Alice was unable to comprehend such a gargantuan statement from such a slip of a lad, so he countered with,

'What the fuck could you do?'

He turned his head from left to right for an underlining of his statement from the ever growing family of eyes that focused on the situation. He found no friends in the crowd, they never liked Alice Cooper either, but this was a good opportunity for them to see what this doorman was made of. Raf sensed that talking distance was running low, lined up Alice with a right, then firmly told the biker,

'Like I said, the man pays the shillings, I do the job.'

The knowing smile ran like water colours from Alice's face, his left hand bunched into a fist and then began an aggressive rise towards Raf's face. All eyes in the room were now on the space that Raf occupied. Alice was overconfident, unprepared and mentally disarmed, like a loaded shotgun with cotton wool balls. 'BANG!'

Raf's right fist found its mark on the smelly one's jaw and the biker found himself unexpectedly unconscious, laying in a pitiable twitching mound at Raf's feet. Raf suppressed a smile, high on his triumph. Big things come in little packages. Raf was a gentleman, Ying/Yang exemplified:

'Humble in amity, barbarous in battle.'

Of course 'good' is admirable, but some people will take advantage. A doorman in a neighbouring city lost his life for it. He turned his back on a young lad at a door of a certain nightclub, having just refused him entry and got a knife in his back for his trouble. This sad incident strikes a chord with me particularly, because it nearly happened to me outside G's.

It was a Wednesday night and moderately busy. I stood at the red steel double doors, one of which was always locked, at the entrance to the club. The outside was under the cover of the market car park which stretched over the entrance like a huge concrete umbrella. To the far left were steps leading down to the market and precinct, which G's is stilted over. In front and to the right of the door were more steps leading to the car park above and down a slope to the circular car park that perched on the roof of the Coventry market. Below the end of the concrete umbrella sat the four foot steel rail which stood facing the car park in front and the market stalls below. The magnolia painted walls to the right of the door that lead up to the stairs also hid the infamous G's video camera which had two viewing screens; one in the cloakroom, just inside the door and another with a recorder in the managers office, which lay right through the glass door which separated the club and reception.

The two young lads came up the stairs from the precinct and along to the door at which I stood. Both were dressed like twins in high Dr Martin boots, drainpipe jeans, white shirts, red braces and 'Belsen' hair styles. I didn't/don't like skinheads much, at least not the racist policies they pushed, but on this door, in this job, I have to be impartial and push my own personal beliefs to one side and hide my own prejudice. The boots they wore, though, were against the dress regulations we kept there at the time so I was forced to refuse them entry.

'Look lads,' I said nicely, 'if you go home and change your boots, I'll let you in. It's not you personally, it's just your boots.' 'You scruffy, racist bastards' I wanted to continue, but didn't. I kept it nice.

The shorter one of the two replied in a polite and articulate manner,

'Oh thank you, that's very nice of you.'

I was pleasantly disarmed by this unexpected polite reply. I started to converse with him on the whys and wherefores of dress restrictions in night clubs, completely forgetting about his taller friend. John poked his head out of the door and called me in, shutting the door behind us. He scolded me,

'That cunt was just about to stab you Geoff! What are you playing at? Didn't you notice him creeping up behind you?'

I was dumbfounded.

'No, I never noticed. I was talking to his mate. He seemed alright to me.'

John served me the game plan.

'We'll go back out there. You cover the short one, I'll confront the tall one.'

We went back out, they were still there. I stood in front of shorty and John approached the lanky one who ominously held his right hand hidden behind his back.

'What have you got in your right hand mate?' John asked.

Lanky looked nervous.

'Nothing.'

As the words left his lips John lunged forwards, grabbing both arms by the elbows, practically lifting him off the floor. John's eyes looked scared, a look I'd never seen in him before, nor would ever again. Panic was beginning to set in on Lanky's face as John pushed him through the club entrance and into the seclusion of the cloakroom. This was the room we always used for our dirty deeds. It was also the hiding place for our hardware - knuckle dusters and baseball bats amongst them. In the cloakroom Lanky went white with fear, John red with anger, as his knuckles turned pale with the tightness of his grip.

'What have you got in your hand?' John seethed through gritted teeth.

'Nothing,' came the whimpering reply.

'Drop it you little wanker!' John bellowed.

A stilettoed, six inch open blade hit the carpet at John's feet as I watched from reception. A cold shiver went through me as I realised what could have happened to me. The hands of mercy reached out of Lanky's eyes towards John's heart, but he never brought his heart to work in Coventry City Centre. He didn't need it.

'Bang!'

John's head bludgeoned into his face; his knee into his pubic bone and he landed heavily on the carpet. He curled up like a baby, not so tough now. Begging didn't become him, but it did save him from the wrath of John who was almost lathering with anger at the mouth. He left him to me. I looked down at him - he was a sorry grovelling state. I found it hard to comprehend how minutes earlier he was going to 'cut and run.' I never fell into that trap again.

Chapter 4

The bad and the ugly

Bad, as I'm sure you're well aware, covers a multitude of things. One of them being 'ugly,' ie. ugly people, ugly incidents etc and so I have entwined and intermingled them both - the final product being chapter four.

Bad people in Coventry's night clubs are not, believe me, a rarity, although in all fairness to Coventarians, they are still in the minority. For reasons of a legal nature, certain names and places in this chapter have had to be disguised. Any of you baddies out there who do get a mention and feel my comments and observations are a touch derogatory please feel free to call around and 'tread the pavement' with me. But before you do, remember I have done just a little bit.

In my time I've met a few baddies, doormen and non doormen alike, but bad with no exceptions, never holds justification and so the 'force' is rarely ever with them. They are mostly paper tigers standing on sugar pedestals. The 'Tank' was as bad as he was rotten, but no paper tiger. His loved ones would no doubt disagree with me, but love has a way of clouding the truth. At the time of writing this book he is doing a five year stretch for a section 18 wounding on a doorman, who he knocked unconscious and then, with both feet, jumped on the unfortunate man's leg. The break was so severe that the doorman nearly lost his leg and only brilliant and delicate surgery saved the limb. He also left in his wake a multitude of other convictions for violence.

'Tank' was/is a dangerous fighter, his claim to fame being his leadership of the infamous 'Bell green crew', fully manned some hundred strong. Probably the most feared fighting gang in the city. I might as well state right now though that I neither rate, nor like them. As 'one on one' fighters, they are mostly worse than useless, but team handed they are a force to be reckoned with. A couple of Christmases ago they ran rampage in Coventry's city

centre, wrecking everything and everyone in their path. One of
the many pubs they smashed up had pieces of broken window all
over the pavement and on the way out of the pub the 'boys' picked
up broken glass and skimmed it into the pub, through the hole
that once held it, like razor-blade frisbees at the punters and staff
inside.

My first encounter with 'Tank' was on the front door of G's
night club. Many years later I was formerly introduced to the man
and found him quiet, pleasant and articulate - we became friends,
although the first encounter was far from friendly.

Saturday night at G's was always busy, tonight being no
exception and the queue for admittance went all the way from the
front door, where one doorman searched everyone for weapons
and another two 'watched his back', along the wall and down the
steps and into the precinct. It was also three deep. The warm July
night demanded we wear our shirt sleeves and my dicky bow was
uncomfortably tight. I pulled at my collar in a bid to let in some
air.

'Big Neil', a handsome, tall newcomer to our door, spotted
'Tank' half way down the queue and pointed him out to Colin
and I on account of the fact that he'd instigated the demolition of
most of the clubs and doormen in the town - apparently driving
a car through the front doors of one place. His name was well
known and feared around these parts. Because of these facts we
decided that we didn't want him in our club, our theory being to
stop any trouble at the door, where it could be contained. Once it
got in the club, it would generally spread like wild fire and need
a serious dousing of counter violence to extinguish it. Most
doormen, it would seem, were afraid to stop these trouble shooters
at the door and would let them in, in the hope of gaining their
favour, but we weren't afraid of them and did not seek their
favour. When 'Tank' came to the front of the queue we would tell
him so.

As he came closer to the front of the queue I took his measure
and to be honest, he looked nothing special, certainly not what I'd
expected. He was over weight at 15 stone and looked fat and

chubby faced. His belly bursting through his shirt, reminded me of the proverbial Billy Bunter school kid with a gob full of jammy dodgers, who was always the brunt of the jokes and bullying at school because of his obesity and the fact that he would never do games. All the same, the fire of fear began to heat up in my belly as he approached the front of the queue. Colin was searching. I was to his left, Neil to his right.

'You can't come in!' Colin told him coldly and bluntly. Colin was the master of bluntness. He knew that with fighters of his calibre you can't show any kindness as they only saw that as a weakness and something to be exploited. If there was the slightest blemish to be seen in your armoury they would manipulate and engineer it until it became a cavernous opening which they could march through without even touching the sides. I watched my overweight schoolboy's face grimace and twist in a make-over of pure hate. His two missing front teeth which up 'til now lay concealed, added to the look. His authoritative, arrogant manner throbbed disrespect as he spat out his venomous reply,

'Fuck off! I ain't done nothing wrong here. Why can't I come in?'

Colin remained calm. His steady look unmoved. Colin was five foot six tall by five foot six wide. His wide R.S.J. shoulders left no room for a neck, so his head sat or at least it seemed to sit directly on his shoulders, like a pea on a mountain. He was blacker than tar and held a gaze that everybody read as heartless, but he wasn't heartless, it was just a mask he put on with his dicky bow. I knew him as warm and sensitive, but don't tell him as he wouldn't like me for saying so.

'I don't need a reason. I just don't want you in,' Colin replied coolly.

'Tank's' eyes widened and he walked aggressively towards Colin, passing me en route. Sensing that his intentions were bad, I blocked his way by putting my right arm across his chest. His head shot round to me and his eyes challenged,

'Get your fucking hands off me!' he shouted.

He was dangerously close to me and in my 'space', so I pushed him backwards with both hands. The crowd of people melted into a circle around us. This was not the kind of man who liked to be pushed.

'Well get back then!' I returned his challenge, equally aggressively.

Our eyes met and held a long battling stare, which he broke with,

'Me and you, around the corner, a square go!'

'Whoosh', my stomach exploded inside. I fought for control and overrode the fear,

'O.K.'

The words came out on their own. The crowd parted like waters at the Nile, as he strode through them on his way to the battleground that lay in wait around the corner, by the steps. My hands and legs shook with the adrenalin which seemed to be trying to burst out of my body. This is where the key to fighting lay - controlling the beast within you. The beast that seemed to be against you, but was really trying to help you; that seemed to be trying to imprison you, but was really trying to free you; that seemed to be trying to weaken you, but was really trying to strengthen you and which seemed to be your enemy, but was really your best friend. Go with the tide of adrenalin, not against it and victory will be yours.

My shaking hands pulled apart the velcro on the back of my bow tie and I unbuttoned the neck of my shirt, following him around the corner, trying to hurriedly work out my game plan. As I reached the corner and turned, he suddenly , from out of nowhere, ran at me, arms flying. I felt the wind of his heavy hands brushing past the air pockets of my face as I rapidly double stepped backwards. I immediately came inside his line of fire with a short right cross.

'BANG!' right on the bone of his jaw, shooting it backwards and shaking his brain. The dark clouds of unconsciousness pulled him to its breast and he shuddered heavily onto the pimpled concrete. He was brave and fought against unconsciousness, desperately trying to regain the feet that had just forsaken him. I heaved a heavy 'axe kick' into the side of his head and his eyes closed - his lights were out. I kicked his unresponding, flaccid body again and again and again. The corpulence of his bared torso rippled at the weight of my kicks. John pushed through the shocked, encircled crowd and looked on sleeping beauty.

'Fat bastard,' he said, then casually strolled back into the club.

My reason and justification, if indeed it can be justified, is fear of reprisals. I'd seen the scars on the faces of the people he'd glassed and bitten before me and knew the type of person he was. If I didn't do a good job on him he'd be back for a second crack at the whip and in all honesty you only want to fight a man of his calibre once, to frighten him. I had to put fear into his heart and make him think I was a bigger animal than he was and that if he did come back for another 'go' and lost again, it might be his 'Coup de grace.' Fighters of this bore only respect one thing - fear.

I did though, come away with a lot of respect for 'Tank'. He was big enough to fight me 'Mane de mane' and as I said previously, we did meet again years later under more pleasant circumstances and a friendship was born through the womb of adversity.

A bad incident that springs to mind that was particularly nasty happened in Reflections night club or 'erections' as it was commonly known then, at the other end of Coventry's city centre from G's. If I said G's was rough, then Reflections made it look tame by comparison. Some say the doormen were on fifty pounds per night plus free membership in B.U.P.A. Others say they were on a death wish.

'Baby Face' was an old friend of mine from school. I liked him a lot, but my goodness, he did like to fight and he did it well too. He was a nice lad, but drink and him mixed a Molotov Cocktail that would erupt and burst like a tumour into vile violence. He was slight, tough and athletic with a 'boy blue' look that belied his talent for things dark. He'd only just been released from a five year stretch for playing noughts and crosses with a razor blade on the naked back of an elderly captive at the scene of an unsuccessful armed burglary - nice lad. He wasn't long released before he regained his criminal composure and found his violent feet again.

Reflections was a hole in the ground, a warren type of place, acquainted by the unwanted scraps tossed from other clubs, like pigs swill. Every single week somebody got a new face, carved with a broken beer glass, a craft knife or a Stanley. The only reason the police kept it open was so that they knew where to find the criminally penurious when they wanted them. It was virtually just a door front on a row of city centre shops that led into a narrow alley type room, with a little dance floor at the bottom that had soaked up more blood than an army of greedy vampires. Even the police avoided the place like the black death. The flag of anarchy flew freely here. It was infested by the 'Bell Green Crew' and naturally, baby face was one of them.

He'd already taken a skin full when he caught a glance of his ex-girlfriend across a busy room. She was talking to a couple of Indian lads. Mr Nasty took over as Boy Blue's face contorted into a domino of jealousy. She was small and pretty with blonde hair and schoolgirl looks. A frown froze on her frightened face when Mr Nasty pulled her to one side. There was poison in his voice and loathe in his eyes.

'What the fuck do you think you're doing, talking to those wogs?'

'What's it to you? You don't own me,' came her brave reply. He slapped her face hard.

The two Indian lads, noticing her stress, intervened, asking him to leave her alone. He was consumed by rage and stormed off to 'round up' the boys. He then armed himself with a chunky pint mug. Holding the jug by the handle, he smashed it to the floor, leaving himself with a jagged, razor sharp, 'glass fist.'

The first the Indian boy knew of it was when his face exploded at the impact of Mr Nasty's glass fist, as it drilled through his right cheek, splattering and pumping blood in all directions. He was unconscious before he hit the sticky carpet. Whilst the boys devoured the other Indian lad, Mr Nasty sat on top of his sleeping quarry and repeatedly punched through the gaping, flapping hole, that used to be a face. The blows were so severe that the glass punctured his left cheek from the inside out. He didn't stop until someone pulled him off, his glass fist, hand and clothes blood soaked. The Indian's boys face shredded, with lumps of his face, nose and lips hanging loose and dripping blood into the carpet.

The next day the papers reported the incident and the surgeon had to put in so many stitches, that he had stopped counting them. 'Boy Blue' later got five years. Just another glassing in Reflections. The joke was, go to Reflections for a laugh and you'll come out in stitches.

There are two different kinds of bad: those who are bad and those who just think they are. Telling the difference on face value is almost impossible. To find the difference, you have to take them to the doorway of violence. The 'doer' will always open it, the talker won't. The doer can 'talk the talk' and 'walk the walk', the talker can only 'talk the talk', but talks it so well that he convinces most that he can also 'walk the walk.' One such thinker tried it on with Colin 'no neck' Maynard at the front door of G's.

Colin had turned the thinker away from G's on account of the fact that he was caught the previous week stealing handbags, always a big problem at this night club. He had a larger than average beak that seemed to shadow the rest of his face and was trendily unshaven, with a white dress shirt open to the chest underneath a suede coat. His lady looked slightly tarty with revealing apparel and trowel erected make up that didn't seem to move in time with her facial expressions. Not wanting to lose face in front of her, the thinker went into his well rehearsed routine, flinging his arms back and chest forward in a fit of exclamation, chewing gum with an air of confidence for a few seconds and then nodding his head knowingly, as these people do.

'You may not know it,' he said peeling off his jacket and handing it to 'Trowel Face', 'but I'm very tasty.'

I stood behind Colin and wiggled my hips from left to right and whispered into Colin's ear,

'Tasty, tasty, very very tasty, he's very tasty,' in true Bran Flakes fashion.

Colin suppressed a smile as he took off his own jacket, revealing his leviathan proportions that lay tight to capacity against the white cotton of his eighteen and a half inch collared shirt. His barrel chest almost smacked the thinker in the face.

'OK,' said Colin, calmly, 'let's see what you're made of.'

The thinker's eyes looked like they were trying to leave their sockets as they shot forward to see if this man mountain before him was real. The 'Thinker' thought, then at an Olympian pace, he ran for dear life, leaving his jacket and his girlfriend in the air and us in fits of laughter.

So there are those who think and those who do and sometimes there are those who go right down the middle. Sometimes they think and sometimes they do, depending usually on the calibre of the person in front of them. 'Bully' is a good name for these types and I think Mr T slots into this category nicely. He really thought he was bad and he also convinced a lot of other people he was too, because his reputation as a fighter was a good one. In my humble opinion, the only bad thing about Mr T was his breath.

My first and only encounter with him was a nasty one, though only for him. Because I feel it's relevant to this incident and probably every incident or fight I've found myself in, I think it is best to explain a little bit about myself to you - the way I talk, look, and act make me appear most undoorman-like, or at least everybody tells me it does - a little soft for most people's perception of a Bouncer.

The main teachings of Karate are humility and respect and I believe that 'with ability comes humility' so the more able a fighter, Karateka, doorman, etc I have become, the more humility and respect I have obtained. Although, as you might expect, I do carry many 'badges of battle', my soft voice, ready smile and general cuteness seem to outshine them all and people just seem to want to fight with me all the time. It happened that often at G's that the lads started calling me, sarcastically, 'Bully Boy Thompson' saying that it was I who picked all the fights.

The 'Pink Parrot' sat detached and regal on this quiet Wednesday night, squared off by the town centre side streets that stood guard on the Parrot like moats around a castle. The front entrance was bright with the shelter of a pink canopy running around the corner of the club and down its entire side wall, offering winter shelter for the chain of night people that lined there. The bright, luscious, vestibule hallway, just inside L shaped past the paying-in office and cloakroom before splaying with splendour into a circular, sunken dance floor that was spectatored by a long bar to its left and a scattering of soft furnished tables and chairs. It had been recently re-furbished and so shone like a new penny.

I had only been employed here a few weeks, so not everybody had yet got acquainted with me. Mr T had entered the club at around 12.00 midnight and spotting me, by the cloak room, took an instant dislike to me.

'Who's that dickhead?' he asked the manager.

Mr T was at the time, the head doorman of Studio 21, which was the sister club of the Pink Parrot and owned by the same family.

He was a burly chap, at 15 stone and six feet tall. The eminent look displayed on his young face told me that he thought a lot of himself. His hair was light and short, his dark suit smart, down to the smart polish on his black brougs and he reminded me of a plain clothed copper, but he walked with the bounce of a pimp - so I guessed he wasn't. He spoke with an air of arrogance I'd never heard before, nor since and contempt pushed out from every pore of his body, like sweat in a sauna. He also didn't like me.

The manager told him who I was and that I came highly recommended. But he wasn't impressed. He could tell I was no good. He'd worked the door long enough to know a wanker when he saw one and he was so sure he was right about me that he was going to tell me so. If he had looked closer, into my eyes, he might have seen the trap there that many, many before him had fallen into, but he was blind, overwhelmed and enslaved by his own overconfidence. He lacked the intellect and insight to see this and also to see that it would ultimately be his downfall. Going into battle with overconfidence is like taking a bow and arrow to a gun fight.

He approached me with the good news. He came from my rear, so took me a little by surprise. I knew when I started working here that I was going to have to make my 'mark', the same as you do on every door you undertake, but I didn't realise it would be this soon. I was talking to Kev, the head doorman and a pretty, young cloak room attendant when he approached me. Braggers and the egoistic love an audience. The 'know it all, done it all' grin on his face was the same as the grin I'd knocked off the faces of 200 opponents before him. It oozed smugness and seemed to shout at me 'You're nothing!'

'Didn't we row once at G's?' he asked, butting in on my conversation.

I was taken aback and slightly shocked by his sudden, uninvited and bombastic approach. He maintained a bully's swagger and the confidence of ten men, though as it turned out, the fighting ability of a hedge row.

'I don't think so,' I replied, not wanting to sound back-offish. 'Well, we might have done, but if we did, I don't remember.'

Fuelled by my defensive reply that had obviously fed his giant appetite, he replied,

'You'd have remembered. I'd have bit your fucking head off!'

I was offended by this verbal onslaught.

'Well, I never lost at G's, so it couldn't have been me,' I said inadequately.

Kev intervened,

'No it wasn't Geoff, it must have been someone else.'

Mr T revelled in victory and smirked loudly, his eyes slapping my face again and again.

'Ah, must have been some other cock-sucker.'

He offered me his hand before the gravity of his remark registered in my bemused brain. I instinctively shook hands with him and then hated myself for it.

'I'm Mr T. I run the door at the studio,' he bragged.

'Yeah, I've heard the name,' I replied.

As Mr T walked away the mousey-haired, tall cloakroom attendant shook her head in disgust.

'I hate that bastard. There was no need for him to talk to you like that.'

Even before she spoke, I realised that I'd just stood there and let him say that to me. My 'face' was in grave danger of being lost. The lonely realisation of what I knew was going to happen sat in the pit of my stomach like a bowling ball. I approached Kev, concerned.

'Hey Kev. Is he taking me for a cunt or what?'

Kev tried to play it down,

'No. Take no notice of him Geoff. He's a bit handy, but he's just a big mouth. He's like that with everyone.'

I shook my head disconcertingly.

'Well, I can't live with it Kev. He belittled me in front of everyone. I'm gonna have a word with him.'

Kev thought for a second,

'Yeah, you're right. I wouldn't let him talk to me like that. I'll have a word with him for you,' he offered.

I didn't want it to seem as though I was telling teacher, so I declined his offer. I'd have to tell him myself.

My adrenalin began a rapid rise as I walked towards the dance floor where he was dancing with his lady and another couple. Wednesday was always quiet. There was only a peppering of people in the whole club. The music ran loud, but the audience was hardly captive and it seemed out of place with so few appreciative ears. Mr T made the best of it and stepped the dance floor with the grace of a slug, magnum of champagne in his left hand, girlfriend in his right. I studied him closely. He was big - could I take him? He'd beaten many fighters before me. I couldn't help wishing it wasn't happening to me, but it was and anyway, I always felt like that before a fight.

I unbuttoned the cuffs of my shirt and removed my dicky bow. I'd left my coat with the girl at the cloakroom, but I didn't tell her why I'd removed it. My legs got their customary pre-fight shakes and my adrenal gland pushed the adrenalin through my veins at the pace of a ferret down a warren. I wanted to do it now, to get it over with. My old friend fear chewed away at the weaker links in my fighting chain, telling me I could lose, that this could be the one. He looks big, he looks hard. Kev said he was good, so he must be. I leashed it with the leather lead of self control and countered every negative thought with a positive one - he's overconfident, he's fat. He's had a drink, I've won over 200 fights without a loss. I'm strong, I'm fit, I can beat him, I will beat him. The four records he danced for played agonisingly slow as I waited for his exit from the dance floor. My adrenalin was making me feel weak, it was tiring me. I had to release it soon. I worked out my approach and what I was going to say, knowing that when I said it we were going to be fighting. He'd lose too much face if he didn't fight. My build up grew stronger. I controlled it, held it back, leashed it. He left the dance floor. As he passed by me, I tapped him on his arm.

'Excuse me, can I have a word with you?' I said, motioning him over to the corner of the room.

He nodded, still smarmy, and ushered his girlfriend off with a pat on the bottom - I hated him. He followed me to a quiet spot a few yards away between the toilets and the cocktail bar. He was still holding the bottle of champagne. I made a mental note of it. We stood close together, too close really, so I tucked my chin down as a defence against a possible head butt, forcing me to roll my eyes upwards to look at his face.

'Look, I've never met you before and you come in here when I'm working and talk to me like shit for no reason. If you do it again we're going to be fighting.'

He was square on to me and badly positioned to launch an attack at me.

'Oh yeah, sure,' he said, and at the same time began lining me up by moving his left leg slightly back, preparing me for the champagne surprise. But he was an amateur and hid his line up badly. I noticed it straight away. It might have worked on unsuspecting 'Joe Public', but I was a veteran in these matters, so simultaneously I moved my right leg back, giving myself a small, compact 45 degree angled stance, hiding the movement with,

'That's all I'm saying.'

'BANG!'

A right cross, slightly hooked, hit just high of his jaw bone as his left hand lifted the champagne bottle toward me. His body hit a 45 degree angle going backwards and I thought he was in sleepsville, but no, he back peddled rapidly, trying to regain his composure. But it was too late, he was mine. I hit him with a rapid fire five punch combination, slicing open both eyebrows and breaking his nose. He covered his bloodied face and cowered over. I grabbed his white, stained shirt by the shoulders and pulled him face first into the carpet - he was gone. His sugar pedestal melted all around him by the rain of my attack. He kept his face covered, so I axe kicked his back, many many times. Kev, who had been close by watching my back, stepped in and stopped me.

A small crowd of onlookers had gathered and whispered to each other. His girlfriend was running around him like a headless chicken. I was on a high. The worm had turned - control of my fear my greatest ally, his overconfidence my greatest asset. He'd trodden on a small insignificant mound of earth and was blown to pieces by the land mine it concealed.

Ugly. Now ugly is all right until it tries to kiss you in a night club, then ugly becomes frightening.

Ricky stood six foot three tall and held sixteen and a half stone of forged black muscle. As the three times, professional Midlands boxing Champion and No.1 contender for the British, he was no wimp. His spirit left him though that night 'Medusa' asked him for a Christmas kiss.

We were both working in G's night club at the time. G's is both a very unusual and very popular night club, in that the whole interior, small though it is, is shaped and moulded like a cave. Rock-like formations arch from wall to ceiling all around, making it seem like you really are in a cave. Even the bar at the bottom of the club looks as though it has been chiselled out of an underground rock face.

Tuesday night was always reserved for the 'let's see who can dress and look the scruffiest' punk rockers. Their emergence from the dry ice smoke that smogged the sunken dance floor absolutely convinced you that you were in a cave. Why else would there be so many primitives inhabiting the place? Christmas week was as busy as usual, with people sardined into the club. Medusa was stood by the edge of the dance floor. If I told you she was ugly I'd be doing an injustice to the dictioned word - nobody should look that ugly with only one head. She had a face like a blind cobblers thumb. Her teeth, black and decayed with a piano keyboard smile, gave off a melodious whiff that attacked the nasal passages from up to ten feet. It wasn't so much the smell of her breath that I didn't like, as the taste, though I've got to say, I did like her eyes, especially the brown one. All of this and she wanted Ricky. All Ricky wanted was protection and a good hiding place.

He must have broken the world record for the hundred yard dash as he sprinted from the dance floor to the reception. He was puffing and panting and struggling to get his words out. 'Oh No!' I thought, 'someone must have died.' But no, worse than that, Medusa wanted to kiss him.

'I...I'm not going back in there man,' he said breathlessly and almost panic-strickenly inaudibly.

'What's wrong?' came my concerned reply.

'There's . . . there's a, a girl in there trying to kiss me,' he told me.

I scratched my head in confusion. 'Is there something you're forgetting to tell me Ricky' I thought to myself.

'And?' I exclaimed.

Ricky's eyes popped out of their sockets like boiled goose eggs and his face twitched uncontrollably as he stabbed his pointing finger hard in the general direction of the dance floor.

'See for yourself man,' he said.

I shook my head and smiled. Nothing could be that bad, could it? I walked into the club, my smile was quickly taken over by a look of docility. There she was, Medusa, scanning the dance floor for potential kissers. Even from the back I could see that this emu-legged, oily rope-haired squat of a girl was NOT attractive. As she turned towards me I couldn't help but wonder if this hook nosed lady had been around in the time of our Lord, would there have been a thirteenth commandment. Then it happened, I caught her eye. 'Throw it back you fool!' I told myself, but shock had deemed me temporarily paralysed from the legs down. My arms lay limp and Gorilla-like by my sides, mouth agape. My brain sent a message to the voice box saying, 'Tell her you're married, no, tell her you're gay!!' But on the way it got misinterpreted and left my lips as a frenzied, muffled, dribbling giggle. The hundred yard dash that Ricky had just set, I cut in half, running straight into Ricky. We giggled like a couple of school kids as we hid in the cloakroom, for fear of being turned into stone by the look of Medusa.

Fifteen years of fighting training and spirit development had fallen out of the arse of my trousers, but at least my 'kissers' were still intact, along with Ricky's.

Ugly incidents of course are not so humorous. June was a pretty, petite nurse with sparkling eyes and high oriental cheek bones. Gayle had an equally inviting body, but her eyes had a seductive, dark, mysterious, daring look that was backed up by her Madonna lookalike garb and a sexy wiggle when she walked. I knew Gayle well. She was a regular at G's and in all honesty, I liked her, mainly because whenever we passed on the front door in the club or in the bar, whether it was crowded or empty, she would squeeze her body so close to me, as though trying to squeeze by, that her lips would just brush alluringly past mine and her hips would push her pubic bone into my tingling groin. Her eyes would close in mock pleasure and she'd say 'Sorry' in a deep, husky, provocative voice, leaving me with an erection for the rest of the night, but it was a job, and hey, someone had to do it.

June though, was a stranger to me. Just another of the thousands that frequented this popular night spot every week. The common factor that drew these two opposites together in an incident neither would forget was Paul, an estranged boyfriend, first to

June and then to Gayle. June disregarded him for no other reason than incompatibility. Gayle picked up on Paul a week or so later where June left off. After a fortnight Gayle also disregarded the poor lad for reasons unknown. Now neither were courting him and as far as I can tell, neither had any intention of doing so again. This is where the irony lies.

The quarrel that would ensue was over a boy neither wanted. June didn't like the fact that Gayle had picked up on Paul so soon after she had dropped him and sent messages of disapproval to Gayle via her friends. When she bumped into Gayle, she was going to give her a piece of her mind. Gayle always put on a bit of a hard front and liked to think she could fight, but she couldn't really and the threats worried her. So charged up by the Dutch courage of a few drinks, she confronted June by the Friday night crowd at the bar.

On the side of the hole in the wall ticket box in G's' reception were three small lights - green, orange and red - that acted as panic buttons. Green covered the small area by the snack bar, orange covered the dance floor and red the bar area. Any trouble in those areas of the club would be alerted to the doormen at the main entrance by staff in those particular areas of the club by pressing a hidden black button. The light would shine brightly, emitting a loud buzzing sound that never failed to send your adrenalin straight into overdrive as you ran to that particular part of the club to deal with whatever it was.

The red signal lit up and buzzed and as always, we ran to its command. Red was the bar area, so we ran through the crowds reaching the bar in seconds, searching with our eyes its entirety for the trouble. A crowd of concerned girls surrounded June who was bent over, holding her face and screaming hysterically. Her friends were trying to comfort and control her to no avail. I was the first doorman on the scene so I intervened, Colin and Ricky watching my back. The low cave-like roof shone down its little star-like lights on her as I inspected the damage.

On first glance her face didn't seem too bad, though my view was restricted by the fact she was still screaming hysterically and covering most of her face with her hands, but something was amiss. There wasn't much blood, but what looked like a big lump of skin was sticking out of her right cheek bone. A closer examination revealed that it was not a piece of skin as I had first thought, but an inch piece of barbed wine glass protruding from and embedded in her cheek bone. The panic was obviously sponsored by the fact that the glass was so close to her right eye she could actually see it sticking out of her face. The skin around where the glass had punctured her face was inflamed and sunken, the rest of her face ashen by comparison.

I fed her with a soothing voice in an attempt at curbing her hysteria, but the more I tried, the worse she got. I contemplated slapping her across the face, after all, that's how they do it in the movies, but the glass was in the way and I didn't want to cut my hand now, did I? Instead I bellowed at her to calm down and to my amazement she did. Her breathing though was very heavy and sporadic. The sparkle lost from her eyes seemed to stare inwards and her hands hovered in the air in front of her, fingers taut and fanned as though exorcising an unseen cranium. She shook visibly as I covered her head with my jacket from prying eyes and babied her through the club to the manager's office where an ambulance was called. Her friend accompanied us. I sat her down on an old leather topped wooden chair in the tiny room where the slick, suited, dark haired manager shone above the disarray of untidiness.

Meanwhile, in the reception area, a young lad with a gaping, bloody, Judas glass wound in the back of his blood sodden head was searching for sympathy and assistance,

'I've been glassed,' he told a bystander.

'So? This is G's,' came the unsympathetic reply.

I gently cleaned around the glass with a piece of cotton wool that sucked up the blood and the tears that had run over the cute cheek bone and onto the piece of glass that seemed to be growing there. Her whole body convulsed uncontrollably and I felt deep sorrow for her. A thick, jellied, black substance that I did not recognise as blood was now creeping from her face.

'What is the blood like, is it thick or thin?' June asked me through the pain.

I, being deadly honest and stupid replied,

'It's sort of thick.'

Before my answer registered with June, her friend who was stood directly behind her, shook her head frantically and I quickly rectified my mistake.

'No, actually it's quite thin.'

'Oh good,' she sighed, 'if it was thick it means the glass has hit an artery.'

Her being a nurse, she knew this. Me being a doorman, I didn't.

'No, no,' I underlined it, 'it's dead thin, really thin, so thin you wouldn't believe it.'

As the ambulance took June away, I spoke with her friend who thanked me for my kindness. As we spoke the story unfolded. Gayle approached June at the bar, looking more than a little concerned and more than a little drunk. An argument between the pair ensued and before anyone could intervene, Gayle smashed her wine glass off the edge of the bar and thrust it into June's face with such force that it broke again, leaving part of it in June's face.

'Had the glass not embedded in her face, thus stemming the flow from the severed artery, she may have bled to death,' said the specialist who operated on her the next morning.

He did a wonderful job of repairing her face, but a year later, the mental scars that are a major by-product of such attacks still prohibited her from coming into Coventry city centre, even with friends.

Gayle awoke the next morning to the cold realisation of what she'd done. Within a week she'd fled pursuing police to a foreign shore, working as a hostess in a bar. Six years later she's still there, frightened to come home.

Chapter 5

Fighting without fighting

For every fight I've had where physical force was necessary, I've had another three where I've won without casting a blow. Bruce Lee called it 'Fiding Widoud Fiding'. I call it psychological warfare. It's the art of scaring someone who wants to fight you into not fighting you. This exercise will generally only work on talkers, though I have seen some good 'walkers' dispatched with it. Also you will hurt them a lot more by backing them down than you will by beating them up. Nobody wants to be made to feel like a coward.

There are three different strategies I use in the execution of psychological warfare: 'the push', the slap', and 'the challenge'. The challenge is probably the most effective of the three. When you are dealing, for instance, with a group of rowdy lads who are just ready to 'kick off', check out their 'number one' - he's usually the one fronting the group, the one with the biggest mouth (there's always one among every group) - and challenge him to a 'one to one'. Very few people carry the moral fibre necessary for pugilism, especially the big mouths and gang wallahs, so will ungracefully decline your offer with a 'sorry sir, I can't meet that challenge,' and if he won't fight, his mates sure as hell aren't going to want to.

Many times I've argued with people and, because of restrictions such as police presence, I haven't been able to resolve it there and then. A week or sometimes a month later, I've bumped into them again and pulled them. 'OK, it's just me and you now, no restrictions, I'll give you a one on one in the car park, that'll sort the problem out.' It's rare for someone to take up such a challenge, especially if you happen to catch them sober. Always be sure, though, when you throw the gauntlet, that you're prepared to back it up if your 'sparring partner' does accept.

The 'push'. This technique is a little more physical and generally used when your assailant is a bit closer to you. I learned the push from Colin who'd got it down to a fine art. It works well when someone is smart-mouthing you, or someone has annoyed you, but not enough to warrant 'car park rash'. With both hands you violently push them backwards. The shock registers almost immediately and they usually back down. If they're still thinking about having a go, follow up with a verbal attack to destroy what confidence they still have. This has worked for me literally hundreds of times. One particular incident demonstrates it well.

Thursday night was a big night for students at G's; they flocked to us in their hundreds. Generally students are great, but a small minority were idiots, especially the ones who held some sort of authority on campus. They used to really get my goat.

Two in particular who I had refused entry were the epitome of this minority. They were drunk and I ever so politely refused to let them come in. They were both young and scruffy and pushed Hooray Henry smug grins at me as they spouted the law at me.

They were law students so they knew. Their outspoken comments ever grew until they verged on the downright insulting. There were about one hundred other students queuing along the wall and down the steps, so they were performing to a captive audience.

Generally the insults would have been enough cause for me to nip it in the bud with a bit of physical, but I was taking into account the fact that they were students and probably thought their insults were little more than lively debate. Also the police were presently on my case and I didn't want to arm them with the ammunition of two 'sleeping students'. The more I tried to hold myself back, the less they respected me and the more offensive their insults became. My temper was bubbling inside and I felt like a volcano ready to push a lava temper through the roof of self control. Having no insight in these matters and a complete lack of discernment for what I was almost ready to do to them, they pushed me still harder, nourished by the excited chatter of their fellow students. The braver of the two chanced his arm,

'Go on then, why don't you hit me, you know you can't, don't you? You lay one finger on me and I'll call the police.'

I'd heard enough. My temper was forcing my self-control into back seat, but I still managed to hold onto it by the tiniest morsel of skin, and rather than punch I pushed the 'lawlord' with the heavy tongue violently backwards, so hard in fact that he fired into his mate who stood support behind him and they both fell into a drunken heap. Myself, my fellow doorman and the once adoring crowd fell about in fits of laughter as they struggled like Bambi on ice to find their feet. The more they tried and failed to get up, the more we laughed. The 'pushed' one finally got up and driven by our mocking, ran towards me with ill intention. My laughter immediately ceased and I lashed out a verbal attack that hit him like a sledgehammer and stopped his advance with the immediate suddenness of cyanide tea. 'Move one step closer and I'll fucking bury you.' I concentrated my attack by pointing at him while I said it. Now he knew I was serious and made a quick retreat, making groundless threats of legal repercussions, his way of trying to hide his 'bottle drop'. I smiled the knowing blatant Cheshire Cat smile I knew would really hurt.

The 'slap'. This is more of a humiliation tactic and like the push, usually shocks your prey into submission without really physically hurting them. It isn't as successful as the push but it still works. John always used the slap but was a little too successful with it. Rather than humiliating causing his opponent to back down, he always seemed to knock them clean out. No control you see. And me, I never really seemed to slap them hard enough to convince them not to fight me. A lot of people I've slapped I've had to hit as well.

'Daddy's Boy' was six feet tall and scaled an impressive fourteen stone, the chip on his shoulder accounted for at least a third of that bulk. He was another chap I'd turned away from G's for being 'over the limit'. I'd even apologised to him for the liberty. Not being big enough to accept this and mistaking my niceness for weakness he started to rant and rave and read me the riot act, telling me what a wanker I was for not letting him in the club. It wasn't a very busy night, with a dozen or so people queuing to get in. I apologised again for not letting him in, and then asked him to move away from the doorway so as other people could gain entrance. He refused and slandered me again, so I pushed him backwards. He felt heavy at the end of my arms and his face painted that oh so familiar look of anger that so many of my previous sparring partners portrayed. I hoped the push would be enough, but it wasn't.

He had a short, light hard-man haircut with round, teddy bear ears and wide E.T. eyes that grew wider with the diet of his anger. He was large framed and seemed to carry all the explosives of a grenade, but lacked the firing pin. Just another talker. He strode back towards me. John, at my right shoulder, was wondering why I hadn't destroyed him as I never usually gave out so many chances. A year later, a friendly chap from notorious Willenhall, where violence was high on the educational curriculum, wasn't so patient with him and craft knifed his features into one hundred stitches worth of new face. The spectators moved out of the way, realising thin boy was going to 'have some' any minute. I slapped his face hard. John smiled and the crowd went 'oooh!' Still no good. This boy's mouth was on auto pilot. He shouted and cursed more and more.

'BANG!'

My left jab sunk into his mallow cheek and I back leg swept him. His body shuddered as it hit the floor that luckily broke his fall. I kicked him on arrival, but not hard, just a warning shot. His face scowled indignation and he tried to get back up to have a go.

'BANG!'

My left foot pushed through his lips, breaking them against his teeth. He still never got the message, so I put it in again, this time busting his nose like a ripe tomato. Now he understood. Inside I felt justified, but angry, angry because I'd gone over board being nice, trying to avoid a fight, but he wouldn't let me. I've always believed in morals before quarrels, but most of the low life people you deal with in this trade have no conception of that. They only respect pain and I do hate to administer it so unnecessarily. On one memorable occasion though, the slap was my saving grace.

Delilah was and showed everything that a young 'fille de joie' should be and show. Her young, pretty face was already showing the hardness of her trade. Her thin, scanty, short dress showed all and hid nothing and may well have inspired the lyrics of 'On a clear day, I can see forever.' The November frost pricked her nipples into little war heads that seemed to be trying to explode out of the blue nylon that encaged them. Her eyes held an empty, hollow, sad look that was reticent with her living and I use the word very loosely. Her mouth that was fouler than a miner's parrot, was only a front to hide her sorrow. The blue dress dripped a puddle of water around her and her tightless pale legs broke out into an ocean of pimples. She'd just been for a midnight dip in the Belgrade fountain and it clung to her every curve, advertising her wares even more than she'd have liked.

'Fucking nigger, kiss my arse you bastard,' was her reply to Winston when he told her she couldn't come in the club.

'I wouldn't fucking come in this wog hole if you paid me!'

She was good with words. Winston, my Jamaican 'brother,' whose hands moved with the power of a piston and the grace of a swallow, didn't quite know how to handle the situation, so shrugged it off. Sensing his inability to deal with her and probably realising that we, G's nightclub, were her only chance of a late drink that night, she about turned and in a tone usually reserved for her best clientele, she said,

'If I get myself cleaned up a bit, will you let me in then?'

I was still mad at the fact she'd called Winston a nigger, so I intervened.

'You've got no chance, you insulting bitch.'

'Oh God, what have I done?' I thought, as she took off her right stiletto shoe and chased me like a woman possessed. I ran for dear life in circles, bobbing, ducking and weaving her blows and at the same time, laughing in a vain attempt to hide my embarrassment. I was running out of places to hide from her onslaught, so in desperation, I turned and faced her, grabbing her shoulders as she came close and spun her round into a rear head lock. I pulled her backwards and off her feet. Her dress flew up, revealing to me and several others who were waiting to get into the club the 'merchandise' and very nice it was too. I was still laughing and telling her to calm down when she grabbed my trouser pocket, ripping it right down my right leg. I stopped laughing and released her from my hold, dropping her with a bump onto the slabs, shooting a stare at her that she couldn't match. I slapped her face hard, like they do in the films and knocked the batteries out of her voice box. I'd heard enough.

'Call my friend a nigger, attack me with a shoe or spit and curse at me, even question my parentage, but don't, do not rip my new trousers! Get up again and I'll break your legs, you slag,' I said politely.

She obviously believed I would because she froze. Afterwards I hated myself for slapping her, but I knew that if I didn't, she would have beat holes in me with her shoe and I didn't want that for goodness sake.

Psychology is a major part of street fighting, making your opponent or opponents think you are not scared or not hurt or invincible. When ignorance is mutual, confidence is king.

The doormen were play fighting in the small reception area between the ticket office and the cloak room. The panic light flashed on and the buzzing drilled into their ears. Three ran into the club to quell the disturbance. John stood guard by the entrance door. As coincidence would have it, the doorbell rang, just as the doormen disappeared into the dark club and John opened the door and walked outside to answer it without thinking. He was confronted by seven rugby players, one of whom John had given carpet burns to the previous week. They were back for revenge. The beer-bellied motley crew seemed surprised and delighted to see John alone. The leader, whose nose was flatter than a steam-rollered hedgehog, with a gritty, pitted face that looked like the sole of a marathon runner's shoe, took the initiative and ran at John, only to be stopped dead in his tracks by a steel toe capped kick in his now, scrambled unmentionables. There was no sign of immediate pain on his face, only an ashen look from where the blood had deserted it and his eyes crossed inwards. John thought 'Oh fuck, my best shot and he's still standing!'

Everybody stood in concentrated silence, like dummies in a wax works. The silence shattered when 'swollen bollocks' let out a lingering moan, grabbed the damaged tackle with both hands in an effort to curb the excruciating pain that had just detonated in his lower regions and slumped to the ground. His mates ran to his aid and carried the writhing wretch out of harms way. John stood ready, but there was no need. Their bottle had collectively gone and they left for home.

John's victory over the first fellow, plus his willingness to take them all on if he had to and the fact that he didn't show the fear, psyched them all out and saved his bacon because there is no doubt, had they all rushed him at once, he would have lost. They probably spent all the bottle on the rugby field. This is real fighting lads, no referee here.

Even simpler is the 'gum shield ploy' used by Danny. Whenever he was outnumbered he would pull out his trusty gum shield from the cover of his pocket, place it in his mouth and say,

'Come on then, who's first?'

Not many takers using that ploy.

Chapter 6

Police involvement

The regurgitated remnants of several Indian meals lay on the lino tiled toilet floor like a 'pavement pizza'. Hovering above, dribbling, moaning and retching, was an Indian off-duty police officer whose eyes came in and out of focus of what remained of mum's lovely cooking. The funny thing was that it didn't look much different now than it did when he ate it, except for a black, shiny, leathery substance right in the middle. 'Oh,' he thought, 'that's my shoes. I don't remember eating them.'

People being sick in a night club are a nightmare because once the dirty deed has been done it is usually club rules that they must be escorted off the premises by a doorman. This is a job everybody tries to avoid because no matter how careful you are in executing this task, you always end up with a bit of sick on you. I do remember one chap though, who was good and thoughtful enough to leave the club before he shouted 'Hughy'. He sat by the wall, just right of the entrance door, threw up all over the floor to his left, being very careful not to get any on his clothes, then proceeded to pass out. His unconscious head, much to the disgust of the dozens of people queuing at the night club door, right in the middle of the vomit. I, not one to miss out on such a golden opportunity, scribbled in large red letters on a piece of discarded cardboard the immortal words - 'I bet he drinks Carling Black Label' and propped it against the wall next to him.

As one of the unfortunate bar staff mopped up our police friend's mess, Colin and I escorted him, with great care from the club. Once in the fresh air he sobered up a little and demanded that we let him back in. We politely refused his demands, then he drew his police identity card from the inside pocket of his sick stained tweed jacket like a golden sabre, sure that we would bow to its power. We didn't, we just laughed.

Our friend was a funny looking type of policeman, with a bumfluff moustache that curled itself over the hair lip it was intended to conceal and his entire head appeared squashed like a reflection in a fair ground mirror. He had a perfect 'Police Helmet' indent all around his hairline and a squat seal type body, but he was Asian and that seemed qualification enough in the eighties to gain entrance to the West Midlands Police Force.

His demands grew to threats as he pushed his I.D. card in our faces. This made us laugh more and the more we laughed at him the worse he got. In the end he got so annoyed with us that we shut the door and left him to his own devices. We watched him on the video screen in our little cloakroom and it became obvious to us that he wasn't going to go home without a little assistance. Colin armed himself with his sturdy steed, the fire extinguisher, also known to be effective for dousing disgruntled punters. I slowly creaked open the front door, just enough to get the nozzle of the extinguisher out and waited for P.C. Hair-Lip to come within firing range.

'Whoosh!' Colin let him have it. The shock hit him faster than a speeding train and the cold water forced a sharp intake of breath into his lungs - he was drenched. We shut the door quickly and laughed hysterically as we watched him on the video. Steam rising from his soaked body, he paced back and forward raging and cursing.

'That wasn't funny!' we heard him shout. We thought it was.

We thought this would get rid of him, but he didn't go. Perhaps one dousing wasn't enough. I watched him on the screen as Colin crouched by the front door with the nozzle of the fire extinguisher poking into the key hole.

'Tell be as soon as he walks past the door Geoff,' Colin said excitedly.

I watched the P.C. carefully, as his pace approached the door.

'Now!!' I shouted and Colin let go with soaking number two.

I watched through tear soaked eyes as old hair-lip jumped back in shock as the cold spray hit him, wondering where the hell it had come from. That was enough. He stormed off leaving flat, wet footprints in his wake.

A lot of people think that fighting is hard, but it isn't, it's easy. It is the contributing factors that are hard, adrenalin build up, comeback, Police involvement etc. When I first started the door and in fact for as long as I can remember, I held a niggling fear of the law, so Police involvement was a bit of a bug bear. My first couple of years in the trade saw so much Police involvement that I became, albeit by pure accident, completely desensitised to my fear. Also, through 'Bouncing' and teaching Karate, I made many friends in the force, to such an extent in fact that if I ever got arrested for fighting, which was frequently, they would help me to fill in my statement sheets or even, on occasions, fill it in for me so that I never incriminated myself.

My first serious involvement with the law came as a result of a fight the G's crew and I had with seven soldiers. A silly argument between one of the soldiers and a young chap at 2:15 on a Saturday morning was to us a usual way to finish the shift. Colin, John and I acted as mediators, to keep the quarrelling youths from fighting. A steady stream of punters were leaving the club and we were just outside the club, so they all had a bit of a glance as they passed. Just another Saturday morning in Coventry city centre.

'BANG!'

A dull, thudding punch that pummelled into the back of my head shot me forward. I turned to the sight of three men violently running at me, their fists and feet thrashing. Similar dirty deeds were happening to the other doormen behind me. Our assailants were, apparently companions and comrades of the soldier we were trying to keep from fighting. On their exit from the club they had noticed the altercation and decided that they would 'have a bit of that, thank you.' The three were on me in a second and over me like a swarm of bees, no finesse about it, no alternating attacks like in the dojo, these people were trying to kill me. Being completely adverse to pain, I quickly exchanged dojo etiquette and technique for basic animal instinct and thrashed my arms in a wild defence, connecting with everything that came within a two feet radius of my body. This seemed to do the trick because they backed off and ran at the other doormen who were already heavily out numbered. They might have had enough of me, but I was just getting started.

The fingers of my right hand slipped easily into the weight that hung at the pit of my right trouser pocket and I pulled out my 'steel fist' - something I'd never done before, nor since and hit everything that moved. The three that jumped me fell to the brutality of my onslaught. My ears registered no sound, I was in a silent movie and slapstick wasn't in the script. Faces and skulls split and spewed blood as the steel that drove me punished their flesh. The 'dark side' had engrossed me and their fighting inclination died with their consciousness. I put 'dusty' away, amazed at the carnage that littered my path. Five were taken to hospital and the Police were on my trail.

Looking back in retrospect, I wasn't proud of what I'd done, nor though was I ashamed. I genuinely believe that if you are outnumbered in a situation like this you have every right to and are completely justified in doing or using anything in your means to equalise the situation. Whenever I feel guilty about a situation or whenever I wonder if I've gone 'over the top' I remind myself of the two youths in the Pink Parrot night club who screwed a glass into the face of an eighteen year old who really didn't want 70 nylon stitches holding his face together, then jumped up and down on his cadaver like elfin frame until we, the doormen stopped them. I picture myself at their feet and at their mercy and then think 'No! No! No!'

I've never instigated violence in my whole life, so if somebody wants to pick a fight with me then whatever I do to them is good enough. I'm not going to be a punch bag for anyone, ever. In the eyes of the law of course, my comments are barbarous and unjustifiable, but as Oscar Wilde said, 'The law is an ass.' You have to fight fire with fire and win by any means fair or foul - it is better to be judged by twelve than carried by six. After all, who will keep your house and feed your children when you are lying in the gutter of life, blood drenched and grey with death because you dared to play it fair with society's bullies.

Back in the club I hid my duster in the hand bag of a girlfriend. The palm of my hand ached from its impact on the heads of my soldier friends. We were told the police were on their way.

My panic didn't really start until I remembered the video. Everything that occurred in the whole evening at the entrance to G's was always videoed and held on record for the police. This obviously included my star performance tonight with the soldiers. Later we learned from our mistakes and would turn the video off if we suspected there was going to be trouble, or erase the tape if we were caught red handed. Sometimes the video player would mysteriously malfunction, coincidentally just as the altercation occurred.

Originally the forces that be at G's installed the video as a ploy to keep on the right side of the Police and licensing committee and it also gave us, the doormen, the opportunity to scan the queue for potential trouble makers as the management installed a small screen in the cloakroom for us. But ultimately the video became our undoing, a heavy rope that bound us to the realms of the law. If we hit anyone on camera, we hung ourselves. We were as liable as the punters and as soon as the cleverer of them realised this handicap we held, they exploited it by barracking and challenging us, knowing full well that we dare not retaliate with 'big brother' watching us. Until that is, we got wise and turned the damn thing off whilst we 'dealt' with them. John always told me to be careful of the video. He'd always drag his opponents to some secluded spot off camera whilst he done the dirty deed. But I always, without exception, forgot.

Three policemen, two managers and four doormen squeezed into the tiny managers office that had been tidied up especially. I tried to keep an 'I'm innocent officer' look on my face, but it wasn't easy knowing what was on film. Cigarette smoke herded the air and daggered my eyes. My brain buzzed and busied itself trying to analyse and assess the situation ahead of me. No one was speaking, all eyes hit the television screen as it crackled into life. Dave, the ultra thin, bespectacled second manager, who was continually pushing the sliding specs back up his nose, wound the tape forward to where it all began. I prayed that a miracle had occurred and I was off camera, or that the tape would suddenly, mysteriously break down. Dream on, I knew I was going to be tonight's celluloid star. 'Play' was pressed and the silent movie began its recall. I hoped it was going to be kind to me.

Initially it was. It showed us diligently trying to stop the quarrel and then being attacked from behind by the unscrupulous, unprovoked soldiers as they left the club.

'Stop!' demanded the hefty Sergeant, whose clean cut, smart features put you more in mind of a bank manager than a Policeman. My heart missed a beat. Dave dutifully put the tape on pause at the Sergeant's bidding. The Sergeant then pointed ominously to the screen.

'Who's that?'

His finger aimed at the dozen on screen, frozen in a second of muted, vehement viciousness, but more accurately at myself. The panic I felt inside was like I'd never felt before. It engrossed my whole body like a rapidly enlarging growth that was forcing all the self control in my whole being outwards. I breathed in deeply, controlling it, captaining it, but still it pushed outwards fighting against me, hacking at my weaknesses with the sword of self doubt. 'You'll get locked up - there will be come backs - you'll go to prison for this, PRISON, PRISON, PRISON!!' The ship of my moral fibre was under threat of mutiny from the minority 'Yellow Crew' within me. I cracked the whip of self control and herded the craven in me back to captivity.

'That's me.'

I answered the Sergeant's question, hiding my inner turmoil. His eyes searched mine for the weakness that he wouldn't find. It was under lock and key.

'You used a knuckle duster,' he challenged.

'No, I never used anything,' I lied, meeting his challenge.

He passed by my denial,

'That's out of order son,' he said, condemningly.

The silence rang in my ears for a long, long second, broken by the 'whirl' of the video as the Sergeant pressed play and all eyes left me for the screen. The voice of ill reason started again in my head. 'You're scared. You're finished. Admit it, they've got you, they've got you. Give in, give in. You're weak, you're weak, you're not strong enough.' - Each trying to hook onto a ledge of weakness, but I ignored the voice and countered consciously 'I'm not scared. They haven't got me. I'm not finished. I'll never give in. I can handle it.' Then I challenged my own mind, 'Give it your best shot, I can handle anything you throw at me.' I knew from experience that your own mind can be your worst enemy and that as soon as you gave in, even a little bit, to these thoughts, they grew stronger and stronger, feeding on each little victory, making you weaker and weaker. I turned to John, who knew me well and sensed how I was feeling.

'What should I do?' I whispered.

'Deny everything,' he whispered back. He was a man of few words.

As the tape reached its climax another P.C., spindly and fresh faced, entered the already full to capacity room and whispered something to the Sergeant. I tried to eves drop, but his message was drowned by the quiet hum of voices that broke out on his entrance. Sergeant and P.C. left the room only to return seconds later.

'Right,' said the Sergeant, authoritatively, hands coupled behind his back traditionally.

'I've got a soldier outside who's stone cold sober and is prepared to come in here and identify the person he saw using a knuckle duster.'

'Stone cold sober outside a night club at three in the morning, pull the other one officer,' I thought to myself.

'To make it fair the doormen can line up and the soldier can pick the person he saw with the knuckle duster from the line up,' he continued.

'Well that's really fair,' said the manager in my defence, 'Geoff's the only white doorman working here, so this soldier chappy isn't going to find it difficult, is he?'

The battlefield inside me still raged, 'Be strong, be strong, you can handle it.' John, suspecting it was all a ploy to bluff me into saying I used the 'duster' said,

'Go on then, bring him in.'

The Sergeant's eyes remained stern, not betraying his ploy.

'Bring him in,' the Sergeant ordered the P.C, who immediately left the room. We waited in cold anticipation. The ticking of the wall clock magnified itself a thousand fold, 'TICK TOCK, TICK

TOCK, TICK TOCK!' like a sledgehammer hitting my skull from the inside. I remained outwardly calm, practising the 'Duck syndrome' - calm and graceful above the waters, going like the clappers underneath. It was just another game, where any visual weakness shown loses you points until enough points are accumulated by yourself or your opponent to ensure victory.

The P.C. re-entered the room alone,

'I just missed him Serge, they've took him down the hospital.'

He lied badly. John smiled broadly. I sighed relief inside.

My own accumulation of points was growing steadily. One thing was for sure, the video recording and the soldier's statement, if in fact they had made statements, wouldn't be enough to secure a prosecution against me. If it was enough, they wouldn't be spending the time and energy trying to get my admission and they most definitely would have charged me by now and locked me up in a little, cold, stone cell without the blanket you always ask for but never get. Instead I was alone with the 'keep him separated from his mates until he cracks' ploy, in a rather large conference type room in Little Park Police station.

I'd been here for an hour.

'We're not arresting you. We'd just like you to come to the station voluntarily, to make a statement,' I was told rather unconvincingly.

John and Colin were in easy street. They'd done their fighting off camera, so they were being questioned about what I'd done, rather than what they'd done. I was the fish they wanted to net, but unless I took the bait, bit the hook and confessed, they had little chance of it. All the camera showed clearly was be being viciously attacked by several people and then retaliating. Although the Police knew I was wearing 'steel' they never had enough evidence to prove it. The supposed statements from the soldiers would cut little ice in court because they had blatantly and obviously instigated the whole incident. So all I had to do was stay calm and deny til I was blue in the face.

The psyching out process had begun as I said with the 'silent treatment' separating me from the moral support of my mates and leaving me with nothing to occupy my mind, in the hope that I would become lonely and despondent and snatch at the first way out they offered me. Having been an avid follower of 'The Bill' I knew the score and wasn't having any of it.

To occupy my mind and stop the rot before it had a chance to set in, I read all the notices on the walls of this coldly decored, almost empty room. The up and coming Policeman's Ball, union meeting, courses, promotion exams etc adorned the walls. I read every word to break the boredom. Then the tiles on the floor. How many across? Thirty. How many in length? Eighty nine. How many in total? Two thousand, six hundred and seventy. How many damaged tiles? Twelve. What percentage of total tiles are broken? Twenty two point two per cent. How many paces in the width of the room? Then the length. 'Papillon' got away with it for years in solitary confinement, so I was sure I could do it here, for one night. Thoughts of my three beautiful daughters at home kept trying to sympathise their way into my mind, but hard as it was, I had to push them back out again. These were the thoughts that were the absolute inspiration of loneliness, so they had to go. Better to think of notices, tiles and other inanimate, emotionless objects. Every attempted infiltration was mercilessly battered back. Mind control was of the essence. I remembered a favourite paragraph from a book I'd once read. I recited it again and again in my mind to inspire strength and sooth my mental pain:

'To think bad thoughts is really the easiest thing in the world. If you leave your mind to itself it will spiral you down into ever increasing unhappiness. To think good thoughts however, requires effort. This is one of the things that training and discipline are about. So teach your mind to dwell on sweet perfumes, the touch of silk, tender rain drops against the Shoji, the tranquillity of dawn, then at length you won't have to make such an effort and you will be of value to yourself.'

My concentration was interrupted by the entrance of a P.C. He was, it seemed to be the good cop in the 'Good cop, bad cop' routine. He was to lull me in and make me believe he was my friend, to promise me his help and offer me his advise in the hope that I'd tell all and promise absolutely that he'd help me, even though he shouldn't really.

'Hello Geoff,' said the soft, comforting voice that was ever so inviting after so long a silence.

'Hello,' I replied, equally nice.

'Look Geoff,' he started the routine that he'd learnt at Ryton and perfected in the bathroom mirror at home, even he liked the character he was portraying, 'I shouldn't really be telling you this, but you seem a nice bloke to me, not like those bastards you 'dustered'. I know they deserved all the pain you gave them, so I want to try and help you. You're not doing yourself any favours denying that you used a duster, Geoff, it's all on video anyway, so you might as well admit it. Then we can all go home. Just admit it. You could be home in bed in an hour.'

'Yes' I thought, 'a prison bed if I admit that. Look at me,' I felt like saying, 'do I look like the kind of arsehole who is going to believe that crap? You must think that I came up the lock in a bubble.' I didn't want to burst his bubble, nor hurt his feelings because he seemed like a nice bloke as well, so I played him at his own game - only better.

'I really appreciate you trying to help me mate,' I lied. 'It's really nice of you to be so concerned, but there's no point in me admitting to something that I didn't do now, is there?'

He looked puzzled and bemused by my reply. 'I can't understand it,' he must have thought, 'it worked so well at police training college.'

'No, I suppose you're right,' he conceded.

Me and an empty room again. I began more recitations, observations and analyses, anything to fill the time. Fifteen minutes, half an hour, forty-five minutes, an hour, then P.C. No 2, the second half of the 'Good cop, bad cop' routine, entered the room. Another spindly character. Has the West Midlands Police force got the monopoly on spindliness? It seemed so. His meticulously smart uniform shone with authority. The silver shined buttons glowed like light houses in a black sea; his shoes shone the shining of a brass bell; his thin ghostly face, the result of night shift working, looked as though it was made of dough with two perfectly formed oval indentations as eyes and his bold head shone louder than his shoes. The hard Belfast voice attacked me,

'You do realise the gravity of the offence you've committed, I hope.'

I never answered. I'd seen this bit on telly as well, so I knew my rights. If I didn't want to answer I didn't have to. He thrust a piece of paper towards me with the malice of a challenge to 'fight at dawn sir.'

'Fill this statement form in, detailing, in your own words, exactly what happened tonight,' he said. His face was hard, like a statute, devoid of feeling and emotion. 'He'd obviously been practising in the bathroom mirror as well,' I thought. He handed me a blue biro with a top that hadn't been chewed - the first outside of a stationer's that I'd ever seen. I began to write on the hard wooden desk that lay redundant and forlorn in the corner of the room.

'Did you know that using a knuckle duster constitutes a charge of section 18 wounding with intent, which in turn carries a five year prison sentence?' he interrupted.

What was this, a quiz?

'Not if you haven't used one it doesn't,' I replied, defiantly, without raising my head from my writing or breaking the run of my biro that was busy putting my lies into print. My truculence angered him.

'There's a young soldier and his girl friend in the other room who have made a statement to the effect that you did use a knuckle duster. The doctor at the hospital said the wounds, of which there are many, are conducent with being hit with a metal object. You know you used it, I know you used it and I'm going to prove it.'

So much evidence and no arrest. If he had anything concrete on me he wouldn't be stood here trying to convince me he had. He'd be shackling me into the cells. I shrugged my shoulders, feigning disconcern, then carried on writing my statement, carefully, to put down the most basic lies. Less to remember if they should decide to cross question me.

'Your mate's an animal,' the Sergeant told Colin, in the small, bleak, cold interview room down the corridor from me. Colin drank his hot tea that warmed his insides and pushed millions of little goose pimples out onto the surface of his skin, causing an involuntary shake to run through his whole body.

'You have to be in this game,' Colin replied, matter of factly.

'Yes, but he went over the top a bit didn't he? He can't just take a punch and give one back. Oh no, he has to hospitalise everyone,' said the Sergeant. 'He's an animal.'

Colin felt a smile of pride rising in his lips, but suppressed it. It's not cool to smile.

'No, he's just good at his job,' Colin concluded.

Her hair was tied back neatly in a bun, highlighting her handsome features - the navy blue woollen ribbed West Midlands Police jumper curved around her tight hip line, hiding her slight pouch. She had been a detective constable for some time now and knew the ropes. She'd seen the video and also had to suffer the insults of the loud, cursing soldiers who tried badly to hide their embarrassment at being hammered by us by taking it on the Police via loud bursts of,

'It's not us you want to be arresting, it's them fucking doormen. You're fucking useless,' etc.

She knew the worth of a good doorman and if the truth be known, she was glad the soldiers were taught a lesson.

'He's a bit handy, your mate,' she said to John, in the next room down from Colin.

John smiled. 'He should be,' he thought, 'I taught him.'

'Yeah, he don't mess about,' he replied. She smiled.

'I noticed.'

In yet another interview room, not too far away, soldier No. 1 was being interviewed, his head shaved and stitched like laces in a boot. He was not a happy man.

'This is bang out of order. That bastard used steel on me. Haven't I got any rights?'

The P.C., tired and pissed off by all the shit this man had been feeding him all night, ignored him and on the other side of the school-like interview desk, carried on head down, finishing writing his report on the interview. The back of his blue cotton shirt was alight with the early morning sunrise that shone through the window directly behind me. His rib cage expanded with a 'Thank fuck, it's nearly home time' sigh. Soldier one, not happy at being ignored, went into his old soldier routine.

'I fought for my country you know. I was in the Falklands, I don't have to take this shit.'

P.C. lifted his head from his report and ceased writing. He was not impressed,

'You may have took the Falklands,' he told the soldier belittlingly, 'but you never done very well at G's, did you?'

'That shut him up,' thought the P.C. forcing back a smile.

Colin, John, myself, the Sergeant, W.D.C. and 'Good cop, bad cop' all stood in the room that had been my prison for a long, long night. Meaningless banter passed between us. The Sergeant, knowing he couldn't pin the duster charge on me because of insufficient evidence and knowing that he was going to have to let me go, tried to convince us that he was on our side all along,

'Lads, I think I might be able to get you off with this one. I've looked at the video again and it is obvious to me and to everyone else that you were not the instigators of this blood bath. I have told the soldiers they can, if they wish, bring charges against you, but if they do decide to, we the Police will bring charges against them, which I know they don't want, because if we bring charges against them, then so will their superiors in the military. Then they will be in deep shit. I've left them ten minutes to decide.'

The air was filled with a silent relief that was almost palpable.

'Do you lads work in the day?' asked W.D.C.

Colin was first to answer,

'I'm a welder.'

She looked a John.

'Sheet metal worker,' said John.

Then she looked at me. Colin and John started laughing. The W.D.C. looked puzzled.

'Have I missed something?' she asked.

John, still laughing, put her out of her misery,

'Geoff's a Karate instructor. He teaches people self control. Only thing is, is he's got none himself.

Our laughter was cut short by the 'tring' of the telephone in the next office. The Sergeant went to answer it. He came back only seconds alter, his expression giving nothing away.

'O.K. lads, you can go now. They have decided in their wisdom not to press charges.'

His eyes homed in on he.

'Mr Thompson, I know one hundred per cent in my mind and without a shadow of a doubt, that you used a knuckle duster and don't bother to deny it. All I'm saying is do yourself a favour and lose it. Never use it again.'

'Bad cop' decided to have one last shot at me,

'I know it as well, you're out of order.'

W.D.C., my heroine, jumped to my defence,

'Leave him alone. Those bastards deserved everything that they got.'

'Bad cop' lit up with hate for her interference. I loved her for it. I could have kissed her, but thought that under the circumstances I'd better not.

That was the luckiest night of my life. When I got home I told my wife, Nina,

'I'm going to have to bring 'Dusty' into an early retirement.'

'Never mind,' she said sympathetically, 'you've still got your baseball bat.'

Each time after this incident that I had to go to the Station to make a statement I got a little more desensitised to the Police. Days on end spent with police officers in court, county and magistrates, brought me more and more desensitisation and also, amongst certain officers, friendship. It wasn't unusual for my phone home to ring with officers booking Karate lessons from me. On one occasion two C.I.D. officers called at my abode for what should have been a ten minute statement and ended up a two hour stay, drinking tea and watching telly.

Dennis, Brian, Graham and Gary in particular, became good friends and later on, a strong friendship with 'Mad Tom,' head of violence in Coventry's C.I.D. Generally though, with doormen the Police in Coventry do not enjoy a good 'Rep' and only a few are respected. A lot of the new recruits haven't got the mental 'legs' to carry the weight of 'Police power' on their backs. Authority goes to their heads and their legs crumble under the weight. They get a superiority complex, talking down to people and generally, though often subconsciously, misuse their power. They talk to people like shit, then wonder why they get no respect, a bit like, I'm afraid, the new generation of doormen. They also can't handle the power. They have to bloat their chests out, chew gum, playing the big 'I am,' not knowing that everyone, including their own tradesmen, hate them for it.

In the 80s and 90s the job of a Police officer is indeed a thankless one, but it's not helped by the 'do as I say not as I do' recruit, who has play acted through all the stringent interviews and examination tests- the lengthy in-depth interviews with experienced officers, always being oh so very careful to be what he's expected to be and say what he's expected to say, look how they want him to look and react how they want him to react. He's just a video recorder playing the tape the Police selection panel want to see, a mirror image of what's expected. But the interviewing officers don't know it, how can they? The role is being played to the meticulous standard of perfection. They should really apply for equity cards and go to drama school, not Police school, but it's not the recruit's fault either, because they are almost brainwashed into thinking and believing they have to be perfect examples of politeness, neatness, with no bad habits, reputations, disqualifications or prejudices. They, in fact, become what's expected of them and when they qualify to wear the uniform of the law, feel their backs straighten, chests expand and goose pimples rise in pride at its honour and position. It often goes to their heads and they become aloof, ousting themselves high and above reality to the clouds and realms of plutocracy, the controlling class, wealthy with power, but meagerly poor with humility. If they want to 'play act' as good, respectable citizens to get the job, then surely it is not unreasonable to expect them to carry on that role for the rest of their working lives, instead of casting it aside at the end of their two year probationary period.

If the people I am aiming at are big enough to see and admit their weaknesses and shortcomings, then maybe they might take a leaf out of my book and start being nice, always nice. It doesn't cost anything and it goes a long way. Read the Bible, 'Cast your bread out onto the waters and it will come back ten fold.'

My own experience of dealing with the Police has been pretty good. I have been fortunate enough to have met the 'Gents' of the force, but even they will be the first to admit, Privately anyway, that there are many bad apples in the orchard of the West Midlands Police Force. And as we all know, one bad apple can spoil the whole bunch.

A lot of Traffic Police are the absolute epitome of everything bad that I've just said. They talk to people like they are pieces of shit and their belittling, belligerent manner sickens me to the bone. I can't understand for the life of me why they are like they are. They should be aware that 'Joe average' on the street doesn't like it. I look into the histrionics of an insult - from a traffic cop, to him an insult is an insult, one copper's bad, all coppers are bad. So all the good Policemen and women out there and they are still narrowly holding onto the majority, will be tarred with the same sticky, dirty brush as the rest.

Two weeks ago W.P.C. was punched unconscious by an overzealous youth that she was cautioning. Last Saturday five uniformed P.C.'s and a W.P.C. were called to control a situation that had out grown the doormen of 'Erections' night club. They entered the club and as soon as the uniforms were spotted, it rained pint mugs, empty and full and short tumblers. All six were battered. Why? Because they wear the uniform of the law. I personally am very pro Police, but because of the bullying, egotistic, power crazy minority of P.C.'s, my view is not widely held.

Chapter 7

Come-ons and come-backs

I can't lie to you, I've had my fair share of the sexual type of come-ons, but as a doorman it goes with the territory. Not because I'm good looking either, as I'm not, although I have been called cute on more than one occasion.

Layla and Lola, for want of better aliases, were, I later found out, local prostitutes who were not averse to the odd freebie if they thought you were cute. They were the salt of the earth, but as rough as sod with it. Both faces painted a picture of depravity and squalor and their come-on looks, high leg-showing skirts and low cleavage-showing blouses were just curtains, covering hollow, vacant existences. The mock fun that refused to sparkle, lay in their eyes like lenses to be removed and replaced when necessary, a blanket to cover thoughts of their shared Hillfields flat where the damp pushed the woodchip off the walls and the baby cried until despair sat on their shoulders like a patient buzzard. G's was a temporary sanctuary. They didn't come here for business, only fun.

I liked them and I felt sorry for them. They were just two working class girls who fell into the trap of easy living, not realising it would elevate them down and down until they were trapped. I'd always spoken to them both, Lola in particular and also let them in the club for free every now and then. One night after I'd shown two lads 'the pavement' for attacking me, Lola and Layla got me off the hook with the police by telling them I'd only acted in self defence. They were prepared to stand up in court and say so on my behalf. I admired them for this, so let them in free whenever I could. Probably due to this favour, Lola took quite a shine to me. I could tell that she'd been very pretty and was still in a way, but her cute face had been 'halved' with a Stanley knife that had cruelly cut down through her right cheek and through both lips. The scar was favourless and deeply embedded like a moon river. Her lips were slightly misaligned by poor stitching, giving her the look of a hair lip, top and bottom. She said she'd back chatted her pimp and this was her punishment.

'I'm waiting for an operation,' she always told me. We both knew different.

When she spoke to me she always turned her scars to my blind side, but she needn't have. If I liked her enough her scar would have been beautiful to me. When I spurned her advances she would say,

'It's my face isn't it. You don't like the scar.'

The scar meant nothing. I was married and had children, so wasn't really interested. In another life, maybe, but she was very vivacious and had the look of experience that tingled my loins at just the thought. Every time she came to G's I always told her how nice she looked and generally flattered her. Her surprisingly shy smile pleased me. I think I was probably the only person she'd ever met who'd given her a compliment and expected nothing in return. To a certain extent as well, I think my flattery was an attempt at being 'a boy.' I liked people to think I was popular with the girls, just like any other red blooded male. Lola mistook flattery for fancy and one busy night at the club she decided to call my bluff.

I was squeezing my way through the club, trying not to spill anyone's beer - an impossible task when so many people occupied so little space. Richard James, the world's greatest D.J. blasted out 'The Greatest Love Of All' by Whitney Houston and the dance floor filled with smoochers, lovers and others. Pelvic thrusts, hands on arses and tongue tennis engendered the sultry lighted wooden dance floor. Richard gave me a knowing wink as Lola blocked my path with her cleavage. Her 'Betty Boo' eyes searched my face and her hands seductively caressed my chest through my shirt.

'You've got a lovely body.'

The sultriness of her voice registered in my trousers before it registered in my brain.

'Do you think so?' I stuttered.

'Yes,' she said, as her hands explored the contours of my body, downward to my lower regions.

'I'd love to take you home with me. I'd rub baby oil all over your naked body and then...' she paused, looking me up and down like a prize stallion.

I was lost for words, too frightened to speak, so I lifted my eyes and brows in a sort of 'then what?' gesture. Then she broke the silence and snaked her right hand up the entirety of my body.

'Then I'd get Victor out?'

My frightened lips burst into life,

'Who the fuck's Victor?' I asked; no, demanded.

She raised her eyebrows like only a woman can and smiled a yummy smile.

'Victor the vibe.'

Oh no, she wants to stick me with a vibrator. She laughed heartily at my astounded gaze and I realised that I'd just been shot down in flames. I never tried to swell my ego on Lola again.

The progression of people, three deep along the wall and down the steps, was as mighty as on any Saturday night. Winston stood to my left. I had the, for once enviable, task of searching them as they came in. Three girls at the head of the queue whispered and giggled, the hum of the backlog of punters behind them loud enough to render their conversation inaudible. Giggling girls at 12:45 am are by no means a rarity so I took no notice. The girls bunched their heads together again, then their combined gaze fell on me and they began to giggle again. This time I overheard the word 'bottom'. The blonde at the front got brave and asked me cheekily,

'Have you got a nice bum?'

A perfectly reasonable question I thought. Her friends giggled at her question. Her long blonde hair, parted at the left, cascaded loosely down the right of her face slightly covering one eye. This caused her to casually flick it out of her eye every few seconds. Her nose was cute and her lips rose-red with an inviting smile. Her eyes were modestly adorned with mascara and I found them bewitching. She turned to her mates for encouragement then back to me for my reaction. Not to be outdone I turned my back to them, lifted my double-pleated Barathea jacket to reveal my 'gluteus maximus'.

'What do you think?' I asked. She squeezed my bum, then smiled.

'Nice!' came her reply. Her friends, impressed by this, giggled again. I tried to call her bluff,

'You've seen mine...how about a look at yours then?' Without reply, hesitation or embarrassment she turned around and with both hands casually lifted her baggy, pleated hockey-type skirt to reveal a flimsy pair of white knickers, complete with pink frilly waistband and a tiny pink embroidered flower, barely visible to my goggle-eyes. My favourite. The knickers sat snuggly and tight on the sexiest little bum that I've ever had the pleasure of setting eyes on.

From then on it became a Saturday night ritual for her to shamelessly reveal her bottom to me until one Saturday, some months later, she turned up with a young man on her arm. That was the last that I saw of her bottom but it was nice while it lasted.

Comebacks: there is a bit of a myth surrounding comebacks. Most people live in fear of them and a lot of people won't enter into an altercation if they think that a comeback could result from it. Despite the hundreds of threats that you receive; 'I'll be back with the team' or 'I'm gonna shoot you' very few actually result in any action. I have had occasion to use the tool of comebacks but, as yet, I have never had anyone come back on me. If you're a fair person and only fight when you absolutely have to, 'Karma' has no quarrel with you.

One particular incident I had with the 'Bell Green Crew' proved to be an occasion for comebacks. I will first describe the incident that sparked the comeback.

At the time I was 'between doors'. My last 'post' had lost its licence due to a petition by local residents which claimed that people were leaving the pub after hours. These people were alleged to have been fighting in the roads outside their houses and making love in their gardens (Video highlights can be obtained through me). I don't mind admitting to the lovemaking but I do draw the line at fighting anyone. Anyway, the pub was to lose its licence and had a week left before closure.

The Tally-Ho stood to the left and across the road from The Diplomat, situated on a corner at the end of a row of shops. The Tally-Ho was an old medieval, three storey building and was always busy. It had recently been lavishly refurbished at a reported cost of a quarter of a million pounds. They were short of doormen for two weeks and asked me if I'd fill in. I needed the work and so obliged.

The Friday went without incident but the Saturday would prove to be a night that I would never forget. One of the Bell Green boys was on his stag night and as the Tally-Ho was their local it was inevitable that they would all end up in there. In every pub that they went into that night, one hundred plus all told, they caused trouble. Intimidating the doormen, throwing beer over people (the police included) and generally having the run of the town were all in a night's work for these lads.

As I said before, I don't rate the members of the Bell Green gang as individual fighters but as a team they are a force to be reckoned with. When they arrived at the pub they occupied the whole upstairs area. I was slightly on edge because at one time or another I had fought with most of the principal members and I knew that they would resent me working at their local. I didn't care though: they were bullies and I didn't hold much respect for them. A lot of them spoke to me or shook my hand on the way in ('Beware the Ides of March') but you could have cut the atmosphere with a knife.

From the word go, they were fighting, and every time I went to go and stop them, my partner for the night disappeared, leaving me to work alone. The wanker who's stag night it was started fights with everyone and eventually caused the whole lot to 'kick off'. His come-uppance came in the guise of an amiable coloured guy who beat the head off him. The boys weren't happy about this and came to his rescue. I looked over to find that the whole dance floor was fighting, and ran across to stop them. Meanwhile my mate had disappeared under a table, looking for his 'bottle'.

As I tried to separate two youths I caught a Judas punch in my face, from the side. I turned, grabbed hold of my assailant and pulled his head into six rapid fire uppercuts - by number three he was unconscious and falling, the second three made sure and he hit the floor heavy like a felled oak. The fight spread rapidly to the corner of the room like ink on blotting paper. Then I saw the fuel that was feeding the fire. It was Mr S and he was hitting everyone. I ran over and gave it to him: 'Bang' - one right cross and he was history. By now the whole pub was fighting and the other doormen had arrived on the scene. They were trying to protect the black guy from the lynch mob.

'Kill the nigger,' came the rioters' racist cries.

Beer glasses, both full and empty, were being thrown by the dozen into the centre of the fifty or so fighting youths.

We eventually got the black guy out to safety and this temporarily seemed to cool the situation. If the black guy has got to go then so has Mr S, I thought, and if he doesn't like it I'll give him some more. I hated Mr S anyway as, a year before, him and ten of his mates had smashed up a pub in which my friends were working with baseball bats. As far as I could see, my battering him would simply be his 'Karma'.

I grabbed Dave, the only doorman who stood by me that night, and we went upstairs to remove him. I scanned the room but couldn't see him. He'd obviously seen me though I thought as 'Whoosh' came a punch thrown with courage born to 'speed' or 'blow'. The punch missed me but sparked a stampede as they all ran at me. I was told later that there were forty of them but, taking into account exaggeration, I'd say that the number was nearer twenty. This is where, if your training was right, your instinct takes over and you switch to automatic pilot. I fired out short, straight punches. (Note: all you kickers out there, in a situation like this, if you can't punch - you can't fight. Sorry.) I felt a couple of bodies fall down by my side so I must have been achieving some measure of success. I couldn't see any individual faces. There were so many they seemed to blend together like bricks in a wall. Violent, deafening noise and punches rained in on me and glasses bounced off my head.

Crash! They ran me backwards into a table full of people and drinks and I was down. Bang! I felt my lights going from a punch to my jaw but I got up and carried on fighting. Crash! Again through more tables, this time on my belly. More punches, more kicks. I felt my lights going again but I wouldn't let myself stop. To build a strong spirit, Karate had taught me, you must learn to be knocked down seven time and get up eight. Panic was setting in because I couldn't get off my belly but I pushed it aside. I was being crushed but managed to force my way to my feet again to continue to attack this faceless foe. I felt an arm around my waist pulling me out of the thick of the violence. Dave had risked his neck to pull me out. Bam, an off-duty doorman, jumped in to help me, then Rob ran in front of me, his back protecting me.

'Do you want some help, Geoff?' he asked. I really admired him for his guts. Bam stood between me and the screaming mob. Mr S's brother was at the front, pointing and threatening. He was tall and lean with his front teeth missing. I caught his eye.

'Me and you then,' I challenged. He backed off, still pointing and shouting. I shouted again, 'Me and you. Outside. One on one.'

He heard but pretended he hadn't and disappeared into the crowd. The crowd, now without a leader, dissipated.

I was breathing heavily, my shirt completely buttonless. My face felt puffy from many, many blows. Blood was gushing from the glass wound in my right hand, my head bled into my hair from two more superficial cuts. I wrapped my shirt around my hand to stem the flow of blood from it, then took stock of the mayhem around me. Glass, tables and bottles everywhere (£3000 in broken glass alone), a couple of weeping girls being comforted by their boyfriends. I was comforted by the fact that I was still alive.

We made our way down to the main door. Dave gave me his cardigan to cover my naked torso. The manager came over and checked my hand.

'You'll need stitches in that. You'd better go down the hospital,' he said.

'No,' I said, determined, 'I'm not moving out of here 'til the end of the night.'

'You'll have to get it looked at. It's a bad cut,' he insisted.

'You've got no chance,' I replied. 'I'm not leaving here 'til the end of the shift.'

'Alright,' he relented, 'but left my wife bandage it for you.'

Bam approached me, impressed.

'They couldn't put you away, Geoff. They were dropping off from the back when I jumped in.' At first I was flattered, then I laughed.

'You owed me that one, Bam, from the time I helped you outside G's.'

No sooner had I spoke than Mr S's brother and three mates walked down the stairs and began to leave. He looked at me as if to say 'there will be another time' but as far as I was concerned that time was now. I followed them outside. As I followed them out, two lads on the door, whose names escape me, locked me out and I was alone.

'Hey!' I called to Mr S, 'I want a word.' All four of them turned to face me. 'You were such a bigmouth in there. How about you and me, around the corner now?' I challenged.

He went pale and was gobsmacked.

'No, man. I can't guarantee my safety around there. Your mates you know.' His feeble excuse angered me.

'What fucking mates? They've locked me out.' He looked at the closed door, then back at me. His mates turned away: now he was alone. He tried to maintain his cool but his fear shone like a neon light.

'No man, another time.' I was going to hit him but humiliation would hurt him more.

'Never mind another time,' I said, rubbing salt into the wound, 'Now. Me and you. Leave your mates here and we'll go around the corner and do it.' He shook his head and slowly disappeared up his own arsehole.

The next day, when I'd had time to think, I decided that someone would have to be made an example of and, seeing that it was Mr S who started the stampede on me then it was he who would be made an example of. I didn't like him anyway. As coincidence would have it, he worked in the same factory as me only he was on nights and I was on days. He'd made the fatal mistake of messing on his own doorstep.

I knew that his shift started at nine o'clock on the Monday night and so decided that this would be the time of our 'meeting'.

Monday night saw me sitting in my car opposite the factory, lying in wait. Nine o'clock came: no Mr S. Nine fifteen: still not there. I wondered if he'd started early and I'd missed him so I walked into the factory and asked for him. He hadn't turned up.

Tuesday night again I lay in wait. A shiver ran through my body. I was about to give this man a chance that he didn't deserve: a one on one, mane de mane, a square go, a straightener. My title was up for grabs. I was risking all for what seemed like nothing but it wasn't nothing - it was everything.

It wasn't enough that I'd stood up to him on Saturday when everyone else had paled into insignificance - I had to show him that I was not a man to mess with. Yes, I'm only human, and if the numbers are against me you can take a cheap shot and I can be beaten, but don't think that will be the end of it...I'll be back again and again like a bad penny. I'll turn up at your local pub or corner shop. I'll wander around your area or turn up on your doorstep when you're having tea with your mum, or, if you've really upset me, I might have to turn up at your job. These people love to take cheap shots to intimidate, harass and worry their foe, but they absolutely hate it when they get some back.

Nine o' clock was approaching with the speed of a three legged tortoise, but I could handle time distortion - we were brothers in arms. The darkness seemed to be magnified by the confinement of my gold Cortina and the pressure was trying to gnaw through the ropes of my will, but it would take strong teeth to bite through ropes entwined with steel and hardened by justification. I could lose and shake the hand of my victor, but I could never give in.

Red Lane lay emptier than a vagrant's pocket, bar the odd passing motor. The terraced houses on my left looked warm and inviting. In the distance I spied the tall silhouette of a young man, a worried young man. My heart rate increased. Was it him? He came closer. I was still unsure. Closer still. Yes, it was him. Say your prayers, Mr S, you're going to be tomorrow's news.

I watched him as he came closer. Every few yards he looked nervously behind and around him. I put on my black cap and in true spy fashion turned up the collar of my coat. I climbed out of the car and locked the door. At first he didn't notice me leaning against the lamp-post opposite the factory. As I stepped out into the lamp light in front of him all his worst nightmares must have been realised. His mouth was ajar and his eyes protruded so far they nearly hit me in the face.

'Hello, remember me?' I asked, calmly, taking my hands out of my pockets. I stepped forwards, but lost my gained distance when he stepped back. He hesitated, then stuttered,

'Geoff...man...about Saturday, I'm really sorry. I didn't know what I was doing. I was out of my head. Look at my eye, man, you gave me that.' His eye was black and swollen. 'But I'm not bothered,' he went on, 'I probably deserved it. Look, I'm really sorry.'

He was pitiful. His begging was killing my anger, but I knew I had to make an example of him, otherwise every little wanker in town would be taking a pop at me. I moved in for the kill, but he ran over the grass verge, onto the factory grounds. I gave chase, caught him up and cornered him, gritting my teeth.

'You Judased me Saturday night!'

'BANG!'- A low, left legged round house just above his groin. He staggered back and before I could follow up, he threw a carrier bag with his packing and coffee mug inside at me. As the cup smashed on my head he ran again. Again I chased him. He ran for the factory door, but I cut him off, chasing him between parked cars in the car park. He stopped on one side of the car, me on the other. He was panting,

'Look Geoff,' he begged, 'I'm sorry. I don't want to row with you. Everyone says you're dangerous, you'd kill me! Please!'

He must have pissed his bottle down the toilet with last night's beer. I asked him,

'Where's your bottle? I heard you were tough!'

'I've got bottle,' he declared, his ego hurt.

'Well fight me then,' I challenged. 'If you don't fight me now, I'll haunt you until you do.'

'Look,' he said, in the voice of a frightened child, 'if I fight you, don't hit me too hard will you? And none of that Kung Fu shit either.'

I parried off his garbage remarks and put my guard up. We moved into the open. He put up his guard and was panting heavily, unable to control his adrenalin. I breathed steadily. He threw a couple of out of distance punches. I threw a low kick, followed by a face punch, but I was too slow and complacent. He grabbed my coat, so I double stepped back and leg swept his feet from under him. He cried out as he fell. His grip, strong with panic, held tight and I was pulled down with him. He tried to head lock me, but I pulled free and punched him in the face. His coat grip released instantly and I jumped to my feet, kicking him in the face. Screaming, he cowered into a ball - not so tough now. I spent a few kicks to his face, but he covered up well, leaving his midsection open. I brought my leg up and down in an axe kick, my heel penetrating his ribs.

'Oooh!' came the dull cry of pain.

I kicked the life out of him. I was just looking for another opening when, from out of nowhere came two women and a man, the man wielding a screwdriver. The first woman was disgusted,

'You're a bloody animal! An animal!'

'Be honest,' I thought 'you don't like me much do you?'

I looked down at Mr S, hating him, wanting to hurt him more.

'Phone the police and an ambulance!' she shouted across the road to her neighbour.

The factory security man, I later heard, was also on the phone to the police.

'Come quick!' he told them. 'Somebody is killing a pig in the car park!'

Mr S left me respecting him when he said,

'Geoff, fuck off quick before the police get here. I won't tell them nothing.'

At this I ran off to my car, then sped back to the pub and prearranged witnesses, who if necessary, would swear in court that I was there all night. Mr S's ribs were so bad he couldn't pick himself off the floor. He threw up three times, spent two nights in hospital and lost three weeks off work. A week after returning to work he packed his job in. A large price to pay for being 'one of the boys,' don't you think?

Mr C thought he was bad, but the only bad thing about him was the smell and I think he came to realise this when I had occasion to 'come back' on him. He was a stranger to me, absolutely and completely. The Saturday night that he came into the Diplomat, where I was working, was our first meet. He was with a young, shy girl called Linda. She was a friend of a friend and I only knew her to say hello to. Because she was shy, I always made a point of saying hi to make her feel welcome. This particular night she was on the fat arm of Mr C, who gave the impression via his glaring, dirty looks to all, of a jealous, paranoid, demented body guard.

'Hello Linda.' I offered my usual gesture and so as not to make Mr C feel uncomfortable, I offered him a similar greeting,

'All right mate, how are you?'

He immediately looked me up and down, with a 'who the fuck are you?' type of look. Then, too cool to give a verbal reply, he nodded a couple of times in acknowledgement. I hated him instantly for being so ignorant and garish. He was a big chap, with a fat, ruddy face - a body builder and typical of many body builders, opulent in confidence. Another sugar pedestal just waiting for the rain to come in. The dark side of me wanted to kill him there and then, but the good prevailed and I gave him the benefit of the doubt. I shook my head and walked away.

I returned to a friend I was speaking with and shook me head in disgust.

'I'm getting really disillusioned with the human race,' I said, dejectedly. 'I go out of my way to be nice to somebody and in return they treat me like shit.'

I branded my thoughts as negative and pushed them out of my head. 'It's just one incident in ten thousand' I thought. 'It means nothing so forget it.' A couple of days later the incident was forgotten, until I received a phone call from Mick.

'You know you were telling me about Mr C?' he said, with shock in his voice, 'Well, to stop his girlfriend coming in the Diplomat, he's told her you've been done for molesting a woman.'

The line went silent. I was completely at loss for words. Mick, sensing my anger and bemusement said,

'He's just a wanker Geoff, he's not worth getting worked up about.'

'That's it, he's got to have it. He's finished! Why the fuck has he made up something like that? I don't even know him.'

'I heard,' Mick replied, 'that he's really jealous of her and didn't like her talking to you. Also a few years ago, she was molested by some chap and lives in mortal fear of a reprisal, so that's why he told her that, so she's frightened shitless of going there.'

I shook my head in bewilderment. I'd met some low-lives in my time, but he topped them all. He was lower than a slug's belly. Mick and I spent the next couple of days doing our homework on Mr C. Where he worked, lived, trained and drank etc. By Tuesday we knew it all.

Mick, being a close friend, was as hurt by his insult as I and wanted to do 'the job' for me.

'Everyone knows you,' he said. 'If you do him, you'll definitely got a pull. No one knows me.'

After much thought I decided, even though I much appreciated his offer, to sort it out myself. I would confront him and challenge him to a fight, the man's way. If the police came, they came. I felt justified and that was all that mattered.

On Wednesday morning Mick and I nipped out from work in our break and walked the half mile to Mr C's place of work. It was a long walk and the build up strong. Mr Negative popped up on my shoulder once or twice, just to remind me of the chance I was taking, but I knocked him off with comparative ease. My belly felt weak and I had the urge to use the toilet. My legs felt shaky. 'What if he was to beat me?' I thought. 'Would anyone believe his allegations if I lost?' I knew he was strong and much heavier than me. 'What if we end up wrestling? Could I cope? I'd hate to lose in front of Mick.' Mr Confident, strong from over two hundred more altercations without a loss and another two hundred more where I'd had to physically restrain boxers, Karate men, body builders, street fighters, the lot, without too much trouble, kicked Mr Negative's arse and took command. 'I'm not going to lose against this non-entity, I'm going to bury him. If he wants to wrestle, I'll wrestle like he's never seen. His strength won't help him when I'm biting his ear off. He'll rue the day he ever decided to cross me. Kicking, punching, wrestling, I've been there. What's he ever done besides lift weights and look ugly, the latter besting the former.'

We made our way to his factory. Not many words exchanged en-route, respecting each others 'quiet before battle,' concentrating now on controlling the build up - feeling it, living it. I remembered the old boxing trainer's words to a young, frightened Cassius Clay before his first fight,

'Son, you should always confront that which you fear.' And again, the great Cus Damatio's words, 'Don't panic with fear, go with it, control it, harness it.'

These words always inspired me before fights and when under stress.

Arriving at the factory, a small unit on a canal side industrial estate, where they made windows, we by-passed the bemused receptionist and walked straight on to the shop floor. My adrenalin was now at fever pitch.

'Is he here?' asked Mick, scanning the factory. I had a good look around.

'I've only seen him once. I'm not a hundred per cent sure I can remember what he looks like, but I think that's him.' I pointed at a big-built, cropped-haired bodybuilding type standing behind a cutting machine. I approached him menacingly. 'Are you Mister C.?'

His bottom lip nearly hit the floor and suddenly he didn't look big anymore, only scared. 'Big', I have learned, is a state of mind, not of body - a Magnum is relatively harmless without bullets.

'N...n...no, h...he's not here, he's out on a job,' he stuttered.

'When will he be back?' I pressed. He looked past me to the sanctuary of his three suited gaffers who were now approaching from the rear. The leader, a thick-set, beer-bellied, middle-aged man asked, with a shop floor authority,

'Can I help you lads?'

'Yeah, I'm looking for Mr C,' I replied, with a street authority that completely overawed him.

'Oh,' came the weak reply, 'he's out at the moment. Can I help?'

'Yes, my name's Geoff Thompson. I work in the Diplomat pub in town. Tell Mr C I've heard what he's been saying about me and I'm not happy. Tell him I'll be back.'

On that note we left. Later that afternoon I got, via a friend, a message for Mr 'Machismo' - 'If he wants trouble with me he's got it,' he said. I immediately phoned his works to find him conveniently 'out' again.

'We'll sort it out tomorrow, Geoff,' said Mick. I nodded my head, but was already planning a return visit after work that night. There was no sense in hanging around on this one. Mick, who in his spare time was a boxing trainer, was teaching me the finer points of pugilism in our dinner break. Today, through visualisation, I fought Mr C fifty times and victored him fifty times as I punched the 'pads'.

Half past five saw me ready in my black tracksuit for the forthcoming fight. I clocked out, mounted my bike, and pedalled my way to the 'venue'. I felt impervious to the rain that pelted against my face as I rode against it and the wind along the bank of the Coventry Canal. 'Go home, go home,' the wind seemed to howl. I felt a loneliness in my heart that saddened me, a loneliness I'd never before or since experienced. I wondered why, then I remembered my recurring dream and I felt fear puncturing my heart and my dream appeared in front of me. I was fighting a faceless foe. He was strong and I was struggling. We fell to the grassy ground and I landed a devastating blow to his head, and even before I climbed off his limp body I knew he was dead. I could feel it, sense it. As I walked away from the cadaver, people appeared from out of a mist and I saw death again on their faces. My heart ached and I wanted to cry.

'He's dead, he's dead, he's dead,' they shouted. In the dream I watched myself walking away and I heard myself saying, 'That's me fucked'. The frightening thing was that the backdrop of my whole dream was a canal. I killed a man by a canal. So here I was possibly cycling to my doom. I had visions of my family at home in our centrally heated house, my baby girl crying for me 'Daddy, daddy', then me being led away to prison. Could it be true that today's dreams are tomorrow's realities? Now everything, including my own mind, seemed to be pulling me back. Just as I approached his unit I felt an almost uncontrollable urge to pedal past, and it took every ounce of my will to overrule it and enter his workplace.

The pretty receptionist looked startled when I approached. This was twice in one day.

'Mr C in?' I asked. She looked around as though for a hiding place, then looked at me.

'He's not in, I'm afraid.' I looked at my watch.

'What time's he due back?'

'Oh,' she covered, 'he won't be back tonight.'

I knew she was lying, but if I was sat were she was I'd probably lie too.

'Can you leave a message for me please?' She nodded her head, probably glad to be getting rid of me. 'Tell Mr C to meet me at eight thirty tomorrow morning by the path at the end of the canal. I'll be on my own, make sure he is.' She wrote down my message, then looked up at me.

'And you're Geoff Thompson?' I was flattered that she knew my name.

'Yes.' I suppressed a smile.

If I'm honest I'll admit that I had a restless night thinking about the fight, and had trouble summoning up an appetite the next morning. I arrived at work at seven thirty to find Mick waiting for me, holding a piece of paper. He laughed.

'Mr C rang up the factory fifteen minutes ago. He wants you to ring him as soon as possible.' I smiled, joy inside, knowing I'd won.

On the phone he was apologetic.

'Can we resolve this without fighting, Geoff?'

Spurred on by his back-pedalling I replied,

'You've got a choice. You can either meet me now and fight like we arranged, or you can come to the Diplomat on Friday with your girlfriend and apologise to me in front of her.'

'Can't I come up tonight?' He hadn't needed to think about it, he just wanted to end it. He was sounding pathetic. Out of sympathy for his obvious suffering I agreed to meet him that same night, Wednesday.

He arrived at the given time, sheepish and scared, with his girlfriend. He unreservedly apologised and I accepted, threatening him with 'carpet burns' if he ever crossed me again.

Needless to say, he didn't.

Rumour has it that Tony 'The Head', so-called on account of his phenomenal head-butting abilities, broke his mother's waters as a foetus with a head-butt. He once had a one-to-one fight with a man and beat him easily. Thinking it was over he put it out of his head, but the following night the 'beaten one' returned, demanding a second shot. Tony, somewhat surprised, obligingly 'done' him again. The following night Tony arrived for work to find him waiting for a third go. He got a third beating.

Still battered and bruised from the first three rounds, Mr Masochist turned up yet again the next night.

'Look, I've already done you three times. Why do you want to fight me again?' asked a pissed-off Tony. Index finger and thumb to chin, and through fat, bruised lips, he mused and then replied,

'I think I can beat you this time because now I know your weaknesses.'

This time Tony took no prisoners and left him unconscious in a flower bed.

One threat of 'comeback' was when Tony worked the door for a fancy dress party and ended up arguing with 'Bill and Ben', who must have been on pot - probably flower pot - because all he could get out of them was a garbled 'Obalobalob a lobalob'. Anyway, he ended up battering the pair of them for causing trouble and now the whole of toy town are after him.

For every comeback you get there are a thousand threats of comeback. In my time I've been threatened with everyone and everything. At times, it gets to you, but mostly you just joke it off. I confiscated a knife off a 'Para' one night. He whispered to me,

'There'll be five paras up here for you tomorrow night.' I whispered back,

'Never mind the five paras, how about me and you now?'

He dropped his bottle quicker than an oily-palmed milkman.

On one occasion when I'd put one of the Bell Green troopers in hospital, a chap at work approached. He looked either side of him and then all around to ensure secrecy, then said,

'Ever heard of the Marching Boys?'

I thought for a moment, then mockingly said,

'Aren't they a pop group or something?'

By-passing my remark he continued,

'The Bell Green Boys have put a contract out on you with the Marching Boys. It's gonna happen this Saturday.'

Initially it worried me, but I thought if they're going to come, they're going to come, and I'll be there anyway.

'Send them down,' I said, 'but tell them from me I've got three addresses in my pocket and as soon as they've been for me I'll go for them. I can live with it if they can.'

After that, the Saturday came and went without incident, though I must admit it was a long night.

One of my friends even got threatened with himself. He'd thrown a garrulous youth out of the club for misbehaving. The ejected one threatened Brian,

'I'm gonna bring Brian Watts down here for you.'

Brian, trying not to laugh, said,

'Bring him, and when you see him, tell him he's a wanker.'

Although, as I have said, most threats are just hot air, some aren't. After a small altercation in the club one night we threw out a couple of lads, one of whom on his way out threatened to shoot John. 'Bang' - John slapped his face, threw him out, and told him to go and fetch his gun. We didn't think about it until ten minutes later when Winston reported that the 'scolded' ones were driving around the car park directly opposite the club. We all came outside to have a look.

The car, a white Ford Sierra, stopped about twenty yards away from us. Taking the initiative I suggested that we storm the car, and demolish it and its contents (or at least scare them off). As we discussed my proposition the window on the passenger side of the Sierra was wound down, and from it emerged a rifle. It was pointed straight at us.

We all dropped to the floor - I got lower than the third button on a snake's waistcoat, and if it wasn't for the fact that we were on a pavement I would have dug a hole and had me some hibernation. No longer having a target, they drove off with a wheel-spin, leaving us on the floor, relieved.

It does make you think, though, because there have been cases where doormen have been shot dead leaving their place of work. And people think doormen have a good job.

Chapter 8

Trained fighters and street fighters

Who would be the victor in a fight between a street fighter and a trained fighter? How long is this piece of string in my pocket? you might as well ask. The question is hypothetical and the answer, amongst fighters, will probably never be agreed on. The only real way to find out is to get all the different 'brands' together and have them fight it out. This in all honesty is never likely to happen, and in my opinion such a mindless thing should never happen. It is after all just an ego problem, 'my style is better than your style, my instructor is better than your instructor, etc.'

Most fighting arts, certainly the Martial Arts, are designed to unify the body and spirit, teach you humility and respect and help you to suppress the ego, the teaching of violence so as to ultimately draw you away from fighting, except in extreme cases where you need to defend yourself or others.

I will though, because of my vast experience of fighting and violence tell you how I see it, hopefully without insulting anyone along the way. If I do, please accept my apologies beforehand.

John F. Gilby in his excellent work, 'World Wrestling and Western Boxing' states that a wrestler will always beat a boxer, and a boxer will always beat a kicker, a claim born by experience and documented fact. He also states that if a ten stone Japanese Karataka should ever be matched against a fourteen stone Irish welder always bet your money on the welder.

From my own experiences and in my humble opinion, with few exceptions, a street fighter in a street fight situation is King. If you put him in a boxing ring against a boxer, however, or in the dojo against a Karataka and shackle him with restrictions I've no doubt he will not come up to scratch. Under restrictions the street fighter is weak, but not as weak as the trained fighter in the street where anything goes. Where it really counts, of course, in the street, there are no restrictions. Before I upset too many trained fighters, myself included, I'll add that a trained fighter with street experience will hold his own with or probably beat the street fighter.

Let's have a look at the pros and cons of the different fighting arts.

Karate. Taking into consideration different styles etc, Karate is at its best whilst in kicking range, comfortable though basic in punching range, and completely at a loss in grappling range. Many of the basic blocks and stances are good for building a strong body and spirit, but are of little use in real combat. Much of the training, depending on the instructor, is unrealistic and largely unappliable.

The biggest fault with traditional training, and this applies to most other martial arts, is a lack of communication between instructor and student. The student needs to be told how it really is, how and why a live situation is going to make him feel scared shitless, that some of the big, slow movements they practice are not recommended for self-defence. Most instructors will not or cannot pass on the kind of enlightenment a student needs if he's going to survive in a savage world. Some of the top martial arts instructors in the world have little or no 'real' fighting experience, so how can they teach something that they don't know? All they can teach is how they think it will be. I'm not saying that it makes them bad instructors - on the contrary they may be great instructors - but when it comes to self-defence, if you haven't done it you can't teach it.

Gung fu. This is very similar to Karate in that it teaches more kicking than punching, with the exception of Wing Chun and one or two other systems who do concentrate on hands a lot, but again very little grappling.

Judo and wrestling. Both are now predominantly sports, but are still king and untouchable whilst in grappling range, though like ducks out of water in any other range.

Aikido. In general it is very restrictive to the average player because it is almost completely defensive. The top men in this art would no doubt make it work in a live situation, but I don't see it being very effective for the ordinary practitioner. The best means of defence is, without a shadow of doubt, attack. Anything long-winded and over-technical is of little use as most street fights are over in five to ten seconds. I once defeated two opponents in three seconds, using three techniques, so you can see the importance of short, effective attacks. If anyone doubts the validity of my three second claim I would be more than happy to show them the fight as I have it on video (confiscated from G's night club).

Western boxing. This is surely the most effective system whilst in punching range known to man, but in kicking and grappling range it comes a very sorry second place. However, these boxers are so deft with their hands that it rarely gets to the other two ranges.

The street fighter. What helps the street fighter swim clear of the maelstrom of trained fighters is that they lack very little. Every technique they use has been tried and tested in live situations, nothing is left to theory. They can kick, punch and grapple like they were born to do it. Most trained fighters are still embryos in the womb of combat while the street fighter is fully matured. They control the 'duck syndrome' with expert ease and put most people out of a fight before they even know they are in it. They are fighting chameleons, adapting themselves to any given situation and changing their fight plan to better any fighter. If they are faced with an opponent who is or appears to be a bit 'handy' they may act weak or scared so as to mentally disarm them, then strike out fiercely when least expected to. If the opponent looks as though he has a chink in his mental armour the fighter may act over-confident or strong to psyche him out and back him down, thus winning without the use of violence, or if and when necessary a combination of them both.

When the fighting has commenced the street fighter will, if he has not already finished the fight, assess the opponents artillery automatically and fight them at their weakest range, forcing a kicker to punch or a puncher to kick or a puncher and kicker to grapple etc. So to all you non conformists out there 'divers or die.' I can also well understand J.F.Gilby's theory that wrestlers are king because most fights that aren't won by 'Ippon' usually end up in grappling range.

At my own Karate club we box, kick and wrestle, giving us an even, all round chance against most. I've already stated that in the world of violence I consider the street fighter potentate amongst fighters with the exception of the half breed trained fighter come street fighter, but the question left unanswered is how do trained fighters fair against trained fighters of different RYU. From my own empirical survey and case histories, Western boxers rise above most. I say this with some trepidation because although I do don the gloves of the Western boxer myself, I am primarily a Karate man and proud to be so. Probably the reason for their prowess is the fact that where violence usually occurs, kicking distance is a rarity. Generally it is punching distance or less. If you do have kicking distance, it is rapidly lost if 'Ippon' is not quickly obtained. The boxer's forte is that he is weaned on the K.O. so is born and bred on accuracy. All they need is one good shot generally and it's over and believe me, it's a hundred times easier to K.O. someone with a punch than it is with a kick, unless you happen to be Terry O' Neil. The fact that you are using your feet to attack automatically loses you mobility and the energy expended whilst kicking is double that of when you use your hands. Also, with the hands being closer to the assailant's jaw than your feet, logically it's quicker to throw a punch to the target than a kick.

Everyone, men and women alike, if malleable enough, have the potential to be good all round fighters. But please, if you want to get a good over all view of fighting, take off the blinkers. Having done a fair bit of Judo I would put it to the very dangerous category, but as I said formerly, only in grappling distance. We were having a battle outside G's one night when a Judo friend jumped in to help. Anyone who actually tried to grab him was quickly put out of commission, but in the meantime he was getting battered by kicks and punches that he couldn't defend himself against.

The Boxer. I have fought a few, some champions too, but never at their own game. Never punch with a puncher, if you do, you may lose. I won all my fights with boxers because I either kicked pieces off them or strangled them to unconsciousness, or even confused them with kicks then sneaked in a punch where a kick was expected. My karate, Judo and boxing are, I'm afraid, only average, but together and coupled with a strong spirit I make them work for me. One particularly memorable fight I had with a boxer happened on a Wednesday night, at of all places, my own karate dojo. The billiard hall had been the home of Shotokan Karate in Coventry for twenty years, fronted by a small bar and six tabled snooker room.

This huge wooden hall, that seconded for a roller skating ring had seen more blood and snot than a fair ground boxing booth. The summer here attracted sweltering heat and in the winter it seemed colder inside than out.

The class was split into pairs, all practising basic techniques. I was walking around the hall correcting and observing. Out of the corner of my eye I noticed two youths enter the dojo and exchange words with some of my students at the far end of the dojo. I sensed trouble and my adrenalin turned onto standby.

The drawback of my large dojo was the fact that it was, as I already said, fronted by a public bar, which was always full of drunks. I knew it was only a matter of time until some of them wandered in and chanced their arm. I walked across, not knowing what to expect.

'Alright lads?' I asked, choosing the nice approach.

They looked me up and down and replied similarly. One was about five eight tall with shoulder length, streaked hair and a smarmy, cocky, confident look that made me feel uneasy. His mate was the same height with black hair and a nice, smiling face.

He looked out of place with his mate, the 'Turd.' Neither seemed at all in awe of the black belt around my waist. The 'Turd' got straight to the point.

'How do you rate boxers?' he asked sardonically.

'Mostly they're good. I rate boxing highly,' I replied honestly.

'How do you rate it compared to karate?' he said, challengingly.

I didn't realise it then, but his questions were just a way of getting my measure, sussing me out before he challenged me. He obviously misread my honest answers for weakness. I really shouldn't have spoken to them, but I'm a nice kind of chap and always like to be courteous to visitors at my dojo.

'At a high level I'd rate them equally,' I replied again.

Then came the bomb shell. His assessment of me obviously wasn't very high.

'How about me and you then. A square go in front of the class to see which is best, karate or boxing.'

I was gobsmacked, my adrenalin was away without a leash. I felt panic and fear and I was completely taken aback and unprepared. In front of me was a young garrulous boxer, standing on the podium of alcohol, trying to take away my livelihood. I was a full time instructor at the time. If he was to beat me here, in front of my students, I wouldn't be able to live with myself. I'd be finished. How would they ever believe anything I taught them again about fighting if I couldn't do it myself. Many, many negatives rushed around my brain, trying to get a hold on me, trying to control and weaken me. I fought for control and searched for the right answer. It came out on its own, angry at the 'Turd's' disrespect.

'I don't like the sound of that.'

'Why?' he smiled.

I saw relief on his face.

'You come in here and challenge me in front of all my students, kids and all. You're a cunt!' I said angrily.

He offered me his hand in a friendly gesture, high on his embryonic victory.

'Fuck off!' I said even more angrily, rejecting his gesture.

I turned and walked back to the front of the class, most of them unaware of what had just taken place. I looked back just in time to see the pair leaving the dojo for the bar, where they would brag about 'backing down' the karate instructor and revel in remarks like 'I told you boxing was better than karate.' The 'Turd's' mate was patting him on the back as the door closed behind them, obviously impressed by his valour, not realising that it wasn't over yet, not by a long shot.

I'm like a firework. I don't go off until somebody lights me. I was now alight and furiously fizzing, ready to explode. I stood alone with my thoughts, looking for a way out, knowing there wasn't one. I breathed in deeply. I couldn't live with this insult. I knew what had to be done.

In the bar the 'Turd' was telling all of his brave deed. Tina, my friend, who was the barmaid there at the time, scorned him for his mindless act. His mates congratulated him.

'Yamae!' I shouted, stopping the class. They all lined up with military precision. I ushered over Mark, a visiting Black Belt and asked him to take over the class from me while I sorted out a little problem. I left him in charge, bowed myself out of the dojo and entered the small changing room at the side of the dojo. I changed out of my 'GI' and into my 'civvies.' Remembering that the 'Turd' was not alone (there were seven of them in the bar) I thought it best to take a second with me to watch my back. I called over 'Big Joe.' He was a big man at six three and sixteen stone with digger bucket hands and a huge left hook that I would defy anyone to stand up to. He was a good friend and didn't even ask me the odds. My request for back up was all he needed. My hands shook as I tied my shoe laces. Joe was still pulling on his trousers.

'Come on Joe,' I said irritably.

I was keen to get it over with.

We walked into the small L shaped bar, all eyes followed us from the dojo and once in the bar all eyes followed us through. I noticed the 'Turd' at the bar, talking to Les Allen who was the elderly gaffer of the place, a great boxing champion in his day. He still ruled the place with a rod of iron at sixty two. Half a dozen of the 'Turd's' mates hovered around him as I approached and the bar room, full of people, watched me as I got closer and closer. He was probably the only one who didn't see me coming.

'BANG!'

I put my right fist into his right cheek bone.

'You got a fucking problem with me?' I shouted.

His temporary high went out the window as shock came through the door. His mates moved away from the bar towards me. Big Joe stood in their way.

'One on one,' he told them in his naturally gruff voice. They moved back.

The 'Turd' walked towards me, mouth ajar, it was his turn now.

Old Les shouted,

'It's a square go, let them do it.'

Everyone encircled us like a scene from Charles Bronson's 'The Street Fighter.' He raised his guard, I mine. My mouth was dry and pasty, but the fear, the build up was all gone now - it always goes after the first punch is thrown. We exchanged a few 'Feints' testing each other. I felt calm and controlled now. He looked scared and probably felt scared, looking as though he was struggling to control the 'force,' the Achilles heel of many would-be fighters.

I figured, by the few testers I'd thrown, that he wasn't holding any heavy artillery, so I rushed in with a front leg sweep. He went straight down, but on his way he grabbed me around the waist so he was half kneeling in front of me. My initial reaction was to punch his back so he'd release his grip, but opted instead for the more powerful empiuchi, elbow strike. It sunk painfully deep into the pit of his back and he instantly released his grip, staggering back and raising his guard again. He was breathing heavily now, hiding his fear badly. Not so cocky now, not so brave. A feint left jab followed by a low spinning back kick sent him reeling into a wooden shelf behind him. His spirit left him, followed almost immediately by his dignity.

'I never meant no harm mate,' he stuttered embarrassingly, trying to hit at my sympathy. I ignored him and kept my guard high, my gaze fixed and my concentration strong. Realising there was no exit for him he growled at me and threw a few stiff jabs that I easily parried off. I quickly jumped from orthodox stance to south paw. This seemed to confuse him straight away and I threw a low left cross to draw his guard down. This it did, exposing his chin and I came over the top with a right hook. His jaw shuddered, eyes closed and he fell to the floor, unconscious. I managed to kick his head four times before I was pulled off him. I shouted at the sleeping piece of shit that if he ever bothered me again, I was going to kill him. At this I returned to my class.

I felt like jumping up and down, but thought it best to suppress the urge and channel the energy instead into my teaching. Afterwards the fallen idol approached me and shook my hand saying that the best man won and could he join my Karate class. 'Fuck off!' I thought.

'O.K.,' I said

To conclude I would like to say that this chap was probably only an average boxer and less than average street fighter. He was also a complete arsehole, otherwise, well who knows?.

Another boxer encounter was with a 19 stone doorman-cum-honey monster who bullied his way around the Wyken Pippen on my first night working there. It was also my first ever night working with Tony 'the head.' The honey monster came into the Pippen with an equally obese mate and believe it or not, they walked straight up to Tony, for no reason and challenged him to a fight. To this day I still don't know why the gutter mouthed buckets did this. Perhaps they were jealous because Tony and I were so damned good looking...or maybe not. Tony declined their kind offer because, being unsure of me, my first night there and all, he didn't know if I had the arse to back him up or not. Also he confided in me later,

'You didn't look like you could fight sleep to me, Geoff.'

I, at the same time, didn't want to intervene and overrule Tony because in door terms he was my 'sempai,' so I awaited his lead.

Having challenged Tony and got no joy, the drunk, aggressive and extremely obese ones turned their attentions to me, throwing the challenge again. I didn't reply, just stared. Slightly unnerved by my stare, the number one fatty asked,

'You don't like me do you?'

'No, I don't,' I replied bluntly.

He looked a little shocked by my reply.

'Why not?' he asked.

'Because you've got the brain of a dried pea and smell like a Baboon's rectum,' I wanted to say, but thought better of it.

'You come in here and challenge me and Tony to a fight and you wonder why I don't like you?'

He shrugged his large, fat shoulders apologetically and offered me his hand. I'd already got two of my own, and declined angrily.

'I don't want to shake your hand.'

I was really angry at myself for taking so much abuse off these two 'obesity boys.' I should have gone straight into them. He turned to Tony and offered his hand. Tony shook it reluctantly. 'Fatty' then turned to me again and before I knew it I was also shaking his hand. Afterwards I felt like cutting the hand off.

At this point they strolled regally into the pub, pushing and shoving people out of the way. A young lad and his girlfriend were sitting down at a table, enjoying a drink and each others company, as the bullies bloated past. Number two fatty paused at their table and stared down at them menacingly. He then smiled at the young man as he picked up his pint of beer off the table and drank it down in one go. The young lad looked at the huge man in front of him helplessly, knowing that he should do something about it, but he was too scared. He looked to his girlfriend for support, she shrugged her shoulders. The fat man smiled as he walked away. We watched them walk to the dance floor. Tony turned to me, still unsure of my bottle.

'When they leave, we'll give it them shall we?' he asked.

'We won't have to wait that long Tony,' I replied, 'they're going to kick off any minute.'

No sooner had the words left my lips when the honey monster head butted a chap on the dance floor. This was our cue, the excuse we were waiting for. We ran across and down the carpeted trio of steps that led on to the small dance floor. I went for the one that had challenged Tony, Tony went for his mate. They were looking the other way when we reached them. I could have easily 'Judased' my foe, but fair play prevailed and I fronted him, giving him an even chance. His insults by the door left me no reason to want to talk to him. Fighting was on the agenda.

'BANG!'

I put a right cross on the point of his jaw and although I say so myself, it was a perfect shot, one of those that feel like you're punching into butter, almost as though you have only tapped him. His eyes closed and I watched as he fell, almost in slow motion, plank like, backwards to the floor. Goliath had met his David. I turned to help Tony, but he needed no assistance. His 'quarry' was cowering on the floor, shaking like a lump of jelly. Seeing as Tony needed no help from me, I decided to drag my sleeping friend off the premises. I put my hands under his armpits to try and drag him out. All the dancers on the floor who had stopped dancing to watch the spectacle seemed amused at my fruitless efforts to move this beast of a man. Unconscious people, even the ones who aren't fat, are very heavy and I turned to summon the help of Tony only to find that his sparring partner had got back up and was squaring up to Tony for round two. I stepped over Mr Unconscious with my left leg, a rather large step I might add and lashed my right leg into 'Mr about to become unconscious' ribs. I recovered my kick and punched him on the side of the jaw as he turned his head towards me and crumpled to the ground like a stack of playing cards. Another one bites the dust.

I looked at Tony's smiling face, the spaghetti junction of old scars bunched together as his large round cheeks lifted into the smile. Together we dragged the scum off the premises, much to the delight of the other punters. When they finally came around, they wandered off in the distance. From that night on Tony and I became brothers.

'Wi Me' was the name, I think, of the Gung fu man Danny fought outside G's. Danny was a big man with a strong weightlifter's physique and a boxer's punching ability. His hair was short and Afro; his ebony face had little dart-like punctures in his skin with Uncle Sam eyes and a large, gold sleeper lay confidently from his left ear lobe. Wi Me had been ejected from the club by Danny for fighting. The Gung fu man took exception to the fact that he had been forcefully removed and so outside, he took up a 'celluloid' long stance in front of Dan and screamed a loud war cry. Danny stayed cool and unperturbed. He turned to John, who was standing to his left and out of the corner of his mouth announced to him,

'I think we've got us a karate man John.'

Danny stood in front of Wi Me, licked his left thumb like a prize fighter and raised his guard. Wi Me, obviously oozing confidence, immediately threw a sharp round house kick at Danny's face. As the kick hit his guard on the left side he came inside with a short, heavy, right hook to Wi Me's jaw and he was in sleepsville. Danny brushed his hands together as he walked away and back towards John.

'My mistake John,' he said, 'He wasn't a karate man. He was a kung fu man.'

The other side of the coin of course is the Karate man who kicked pieces off five C.I.D. men who, unsuccessfully, tried to arrest him outside a restaurant. Or there was Sensei Terry O' Neil who scored over fifty knockouts with kicking techniques in Liverpool's infamous nightclubs, where he worked for 17 years as a doorman. I, myself, although admittedly only an average karataka, have had considerable scores with karate techniques in live situations. One that springs to mind is a situation that occurred at two in the morning outside G's.

We worked a system at G's where by a cloak room ticket was given out with every coat that was given in and at the end of the night, the punter would hand in his or her ticket and in return, get their coat back. If they should lose their ticket they would have to wait until the end of the night when everybody else had claimed their coats. If their's was still there, then they could claim it without a ticket.

Colin approached me in the club and explained that there was a group of lads in the reception area refusing to leave. One of them had lost his cloak room ticket and wasn't prepared to wait until everyone else had left to get his coat. After a bit of argument Colin told him to leave the club and his request was declined. This is where I came on the scene and walked down to the main door with Colin. There were four of them hovering around the cloak room and we went straight over to them. They were all in their early twenties and quite smartly dressed, just ordinary, average, run of the mill lads really. When I asked them to leave they offered no resistance and obligingly left. I was a little surprised as I at the very least expected an argument, but no, nothing. I stayed at the door with Colin, just in case. I must have drifted off into a day dream because I never noticed as they re-entered the club and the next thing I knew, they were standing threateningly in front of me.

The one who lost his ticket was swinging his now retrieved coat in my face; his cigarette hanging loosely from his mouth and eyes squinting. My first reaction was to hit him for his cheek, but I resisted the urge and pushed him towards the door, ordering him out. He pushed me back. That was enough. I lashed out with a low front kick that knocked him through the door and out of the club. Colin and I followed them out.

All four surrounded me and moved in. I punched the closest one to me in the face and immediately swept his legs from underneath him with a low sweeping kick to the back of his ankles. As he landed heavily on the floor I stamped on his face and he was asleep. The second foot-stepped straight on to a right hook that devastated him, his unconscious body twisting in the air as though in a death throw and spiralled down to the ground. His head hit the floor where his feet had just been and the hollow echo of his skull coupled with the squelch of his splitting eye socket was heard all around. At this point the other two were having second thoughts about fighting me. The odds were considerably less now and they didn't want to catch any of that sweep, stamp shit. But it was too late. The gauntlet had been thrown, their bed was made and they were now duty bound to lie in it. The trouble was, this bed was a concrete bed called pavement. Back leg sweep, stamp. The third was gone, only number four left. I looked into his eyes and saw only fear. I gave him the chance to back off, to get away, to run, but he wouldn't and didn't. I could see he wanted to run by the way his body involuntarily rocked back and forth and that he was having to force his body to stay put and attack me. He edged forward and I was forced to put him out of his misery. Back leg sweep and he hit the ground with a thudding crash. My stamp was not necessary - he was already sleeping.

All four lay unconscious around me. John came out of the club, looked at the blood weeping bodies that lay in carnage around me and shook his head disapprovingly.

'You're a bad man Geoff.'

Colin intervened and told John the circumstances that led up to the incident. Then he shook his head again, but now he understood. I was later informed that the lads concerned were local bullies and ruled the roast in their own area. The bully always meets his master.

Street fighting is as intricate an art as any I've seen, probably more so than most. Most styles promote one, two or very rarely three distances. The street fighter will learn and perfect four - kicking, grappling, punching and talking distance. The first three distances we all know about, but few have any conception of talking distance. This is the doorman's favourite. Good doormen and good street fighters have it down to a fine art. It's the art of talking your way into a good attacking/defending position without your opponent/assailant knowing. How can you throw an effective punch for instance, if you are square onto someone or defend from such an unbalanced position?

There was the Mr T fight for instance. Whilst I was talking to him I positioned myself my moving my left leg slightly to my left, giving myself a small 45 degree angled stance, holding stability and also putting myself in the best position to throw a right cross, utilising maximum body weight. So as soon as negotiations break down, if indeed they do, and violence is employed, I am already in a prime position to strike without any more preparation or adjustment.

If you feel that negotiations are going to be fruitless any way, you can use talking distance to set up your attack all the same, perhaps by asking your opponent a question, any question, just to engage his brain for long enough for you to launch your attack. You don't have to wait for an answer, you can strike as soon as you have asked, or if you want to be particularly malicious, you can strike as he begins to answer (The jaw is easier broken whilst the mouth is ajar.) Or if your antagonist asks you a question, you can pretend you didn't hear their question and lean forward as though trying to hear what they are saying,

'Sorry mate, what did you say?'

Then bounce off the lean forward into a fully fledged attack. Or feign cowardice,

'I don't want any trouble mate.'

Then 'BANG!' Hit him whilst his mental guard is dropped. A friend that I used to work on the door with would use the same trick again and again. When he got to the stage in an argument where he knew it couldn't be resolved verbally, he would turn away from them as though walking away and then rapidly turn back and strike, usually, because of sheer surprise scoring with 'Ippon.'

Kev, the best right hand puncher on God's earth, was a master of the talking distance. He's only five foot six tall with a slightly receding hair, but he had bulldog like shoulders. His face was gruff, but handsome with a very soft voice and respectful manner. He was very similar to myself in that he didn't seem the doorman type. He was a gentle man of the door, but my goodness, could he have a fight. A classic example of talking distance was when Kev was working the door at the infamous Reflections.

Two name fighters, who were also brothers, had started fighting with a couple of other lads on the dance floor of the club. When

Kev arrived on the scene the two brothers were just finishing off their victims. Kev and the other two doormen ejected the two battered and bruised men from the club, then he told the brothers that they also had to leave. They refused, point blank. Knowing their 'rep' for violence Kev went into his time served and hard practised routine,

'Come on lads, don't be like that. I'm only doing my job. Look, I'm supposed to be head doorman here. If the manager thinks that I'm backing down to you I'm going to look a right idiot. Just come up to the bar and we'll talk about it. You don't have to leave, it's just to look good in front of the manager.'

They bought it, hook, line and sinker, probably thinking what a 'softy' Kev was and revelling in their own self importance. At the bar Kev made his play, lining them both up with a right,

'Look lads, we've thrown the other two out, now you've got to leave as well,' he said sternly.

Anger hit their faces. The first brother launched himself into an attack at Kev, but Kev was already primed and cocked.

'BANG!'

They were both in sleepsville.

Tony 'the head' used a similar approach on a local sixteen stone bully, whose party tricks included ordering large rounds of drinks and then refusing to pay for them and demanding a stay back with menace. He was a tyrant and hated by the locals, young and old alike. Those who told him so got slapped down heavily, that is until he crossed Tony's path. Ray was a regular at the Pippin and he'd been barred from the place on several occasions, but always seemed to talk his way back in when his silver tongue was sober. Everybody was frightened of him. If he was refused an after hours drink, he would flip until the 'gaffer' conceded and let him have his way. He was a landlord's nightmare. This is one of the reasons that doormen were employed at this and many other establishments.

The crashing of smashed optics behind the bar made Tony jump. He was by the pool tables, getting the last of the stragglers out of the pub - it was 11.25 p.m. and they should all have been out by now. He ran to where the crashing sound had come from. Ray was stood at the bar growling like a huge angry bear, pointing and shouting at Paul, who was a good, fair manager, but not a fighter. In this job, in this city you needed to be a fighter if you wanted any chance of surviving. Paul had spent many, many sleepless nights worrying over the bully they called Ray. He'd even considered having Ray 'done' by a professional, but his conscience wouldn't allow it. The last manager to stand up to Ray had his home petrol bombed and his wife hospitalised. When Ray was in prison last year for a section 18 wounding, Paul had felt great, slept well and even his ulcers stopped playing him up. As soon as he was released, it all started again.

Paul had told Ray that he was tired and wasn't having a late drink tonight. Ray's answer to that was to throw a 'Pils' bottle at him, narrowly missing and smashing the optics to pieces.

'Come on Ray,' said Tony, placing his hands on Ray's shoulders to hold him away from Paul who was visibly shaking.

'You'll have to go. Paul isn't having a stay back tonight.'

Ray by-passed Tony's polite request, not noticing the 'head' line up that Tony had brought into play.

'I want a fucking stay back!' Ray shouted, looking past Tony at Paul.

Tony held his shoulders firmly and said nicely,

'Come on Ray, you've had enough. Leave it now.'

Ray obviously thought he'd got Tony scared and tried to push him out of the way to get at Paul. Tony released his hold on Ray's shoulders and let his weight fall rapidly forward. Then from his pre-cocked position, 'BANG!' He launched a head butt that might have been fathered by a Rhinoceros. Ray's nose said goodbye to his face and his legs gave in to gravity.

Shortly after this Paul left the Pippin for a pub with calmer waters and Ray, thinking his ban from the pub ended with Paul's reign as manager, gave us another little visit. This particular night I was on my own.

To drop Ray's mental guard, Tony had 'played it scared' but I decided to do the opposite and 'play it fearless' in an attempt at scaring him into not wanting to fight me or 'psyching' him out. The atmosphere went cold as Ray walked into the lounge. The bar staff knew him of old and they shouldn't have served him really, because he was barred, but they were all frightened to death of him. I was in the toilet when he came in, otherwise he wouldn't have got passed the door. I was just zipping up my flies when the manager informed me that Ray was drinking in the lounge and he wanted him out. My adrenalin rushed into my veins just at the mention of his name. I made my way to where he was drinking. His dark, Sicilian features gave him the look of a gangster as he sipped slowly from the Pils bottle in his left hand. I made a mental note of the bottle, Ray's favourite weapon and got straight to the point with my fearless approach,

'Ray you're barred. You've got to leave.'

He looked at me, swigged on his beer and then looked away. He never even answered me and his facial expression never changed. I tried again,

'Did you hear me Ray?' I asked.

He turned his head towards me and stared.

'There's a new manager here, so my barr is over,' he replied.

It was a war of nerves that I had played before with better players than he and not lost, so I wasn't about to lose here.

'The doormen have barred you and the barr is for life,' I said in an emotionless voice. Again he swigged from his bottle and again he didn't reply. His way, I knew, of demoralising me by trying to make me think that I wasn't threatening or worthy enough to even warrant a reply from him. A lot of fighters try this one, but it wasn't going to deter me because it was all incidental and trivial for two reasons - one, I'd heard it all before and two, I'd already made up my mind to fight him if he didn't leave anyway.

'Are you going to leave?' I asked for the final time, lining him up with a right just in case.

He tried to attack me with his eyes; to worry me; to scare me, but it wasn't happening for him.

'No,' he replied arrogantly, taking the verbal fight as far as it could go.

'Then I guess we're fighting then,' I said, meeting his visual attack with a piercing stare that must have convinced him I was not bluffing.

I decided that the next aggressive word that left his lips was going to be plugged by the callousness of the first two knuckles on my right hand, but there was no need. His bottle went and he declined my challenge,

'Let me finish my beer and I'll leave,' he asked.

This was another ploy. If I left him for a few minutes to finish his drink it would look to all as though he was leaving of his own accord and not being thrown out. This was no good to me. I needed everyone to see that I was kicking him out and that his bullying days at the Pippin were over.

'No,' I said firmly, 'You'll have to go now.'

He looked at me, despisingly. For a second I thought I saw a glimmer of bravery in his look. I thought he was going to 'go for it,' but no, he turned and left. At the door he turned to me and in a last ditch attempt at saving face, he threatened me.

'I'll be back for you!'

'Don't bother to come back Ray. Step onto the car park with me and do it now.'

I couldn't allow him even an inch. I had to demoralise him completely. Show him no mercy. I'd seen him fight before - he was very good and I couldn't afford to show a weakness. He shook his head, dejectedly and left.

With a little bit of acting I backed him down to nothing. This ploy has worked for me on endless occasions, but a word of warning. Only use this approach if you are prepared to back it up. You'll always get one who will take up your challenge.

Chapter 9

Man-made misconceptions

You are as you look. This is one of life's greatest misconceptions. If you are big and muscular with a face like ten boxers, you can 'motor'. If you are thin and polite, you can't. Of course that's a load of rubbish, but it's the way people, in general, look at you. This has been the reason behind most of my fights, as I mentioned earlier, but it has also been my greatest strength in that I mentally disarm people without even trying. With the added aid of a little acting, acting weak or strong, the misconception grows ten fold. If you look a little bit of a softy and then act it, your opponent will definitely believe it, causing under estimation, followed by mental disarmament, followed hopefully, usually by victory.

The same applies if you look tough, then act tough. Most people won't fight you because they believe it so much that they feel the chances of you beating them are too high to risk taking the chance. I have found that the better the fighter, the more humble the person - with ability comes humility. Usually the more pushy, bullying people are not quite so able, even though they may appear to be, they are just carrying a chip on their shoulder that seems to motivate their bad attitude.

This image approach is worn by many doormen. I myself try to play down the role by just being myself.

'Why are you a doorman, you're too soft to be on the door,' a girl in G's nightclub once commented.

'Well, we can't all be hardmen,' I replied. 'There's got be some softies.'

'I suppose so,' she said, believing my reply to be a conformation of what she thought.

Ten minutes or so later, I noticed an altercation between a young couple. The lad was poking and pushing the girl. I learned later that he'd just knocked out a chap for dancing with her and he was scorning her for dancing with him. He was maybe 18, fresh faced, with smart, side parted hair and neat attire. I approached the lad, who it turned out was the All England boxing champion at his age and weight, to try and calm him down, but my presence seemed to make him worse. The club was heaving as usual.

'Look, calm down,' I said, touching his arm in a friendly gesture. 'What's the matter with you?'

'Get your fucking hands off me!' he shouted, then pushed my hand violently away.

I automatically twisted him in to a rear headlock, ready to eject him from the club. He went crazy and I struggled to hold him. I threw him backwards into a mirrored wall and as he bounced off I upper-cutted him on the jaw. His legs said, 'I don't know about you, but we're going down' and down he went. I kicked him in the face as he descended and his head bashed off the wall, only to meet a second kick that ended the game. John intervened and dragged the lad out. As I straightened myself up I caught a wicked glance off my lady companion, I'd minutes before been talking to.

'Sorry about that,' I offered.

She stared at me, amazed, then at the floor where the dirty deed was done, then at me again. Half disgusted and half impressed she said,

'You're an animal.'

'Ah shucks!' I thought. 'You're just saying that.'

'You saw him go for me, he asked for it,' I tried to justify.

'You're an animal,' she repeated, shaking her pretty head disbelievingly.

Ricky James looked like a doorman. Six foot three tall, weighing nearly seventeen stone and No.1 contender for the professional British Boxing title, but he was so charming and mild mannered he was also under estimated. Ricky and I worked for many years together and because of our polite approach, on more than one occasion, had to show the 'Iron Hand.'

The phone rang in reception, my ears pricked in anticipation, sensing trouble like an Alsatian guard dog. The D.J. reported that a group of chaps, by the exit doors, were smashing beer glasses everywhere in this dark, secluded part of G's and of course, when asked they all denied any knowledge of it. They were arrogant and gave us looks that said they 'no classed' us, but I was used to that and knew it could be my saving grace. Just to double check I re-affirmed it with the D.J.

'Yes,' he said, 'it's definitely them. I watched them doing it.'

I returned to the seated glass smashers, about twelve in all. I breathed slowly and deeply to control the flow.

'You'll have to leave lads. I've spoken to the D.J. and he said it was definitely you who smashed the glasses.'

In an act of arrogance, none looked up. Number One spoke to me,

'We're not leaving. We've done nothing.'

'You were seen doing it,' I said.

I gave them one more chance. Still not looking at me, he replied,

'We're staying.' Arrogant bastard.

They were all men in their late twenties, not kids and were the typical bullies, not afraid of us in the least. The fact that they didn't look at me as I spoke and the very confident manner in which their leader spoke, told me and showed me they were over confident in the extreme. I whispered to Ricky to open the exit doors. This he did. I walked slowly behind Number One, put him in a rear headlock and dragged him backwards, off his stool, through the broken glass and threw him hard into the metal balcony rails outside. As he angrily tried to get back up, I round housed him on the jaw and he was asleep. His mates, six of them, were around us like buzzards around a corpse. As Number Two approached me, I kicked him hard in the lower abdomen, but instead of finishing him with a punch, I stepped back and beckoned him on.

'BANG!'

He'd forgotten about Ricky at his left side and paid for it dearly with a left hook that might have been a shot from a cannon. He hit the deck hard and was asleep. At the sight and sound of this, the others were not so game now, so between us we picked them off easily, until all were gone. One of the first to fall had recovered and ran off for some ammo. He returned with a twelve foot hollow pole and ran at us with it. He launched his lance and missed us by inches. We ran after him, but he was gone, leaving insults like 'You fucking nigger!' at Ricky, in his trail.

When we got back from the chase, Number One was still unconscious, Number Two and Three were trying to pick him up and carrying him away. I don't think they'll ever judge a book by its cover again.

Although it's a rarity, there are one or two people who analyse before they evaluate. One such person, who I'd never met before, approached me in a pub I was working.

'Excuse me,' he asked studiously, 'but what do you do?'

Noticing my baffled look, he enlarged.

'I was looking at you from the bar and I thought, you don't look like a bouncer, so you must do something. Perhaps boxing, or karate?'

I was flattered and smiled. He was the first person I'd ever encountered with such insight. Sure of my approval, he continued.

'It stands to reason, doesn't it. Nobody's going to pay you good money if you're not something.'

'I'll tell you mate,' I laughed, 'if everyone looked at it like that, my job would be a lot easier.'

We both laughed. One of the better punters.

'You know what Geoff?' a friend once said. 'I don't like the look of that short bouncer on the door of the Tally Ho. I reckon I could take him, he looks nothing.'

I knew the chap he meant, he did look nothing, but was in fact a fierce, psychopathic fighter. My friend was about to jump confidently over a two foot wall, not realising it had a fifteen foot drop on the other side.

'Look at it logically Paul,' I said. 'To my knowledge he's been on that door for two years, getting a hundred sovs a week. That's ten thousand pounds. Now, in all honesty, do you think he's gonna be paid that kind of money for a job he can't do?'

He thought for a second.

'I didn't look at it like that.'

'You will next time' I thought.

I, of course, get that sort of attitude a lot. I bumped into a friend one daytime in the town. We exchanged greetings and then he asked,

'Are you still on the door at G's?'

His muscular companion looked me up and down in amazement.

'Are you a bouncer?' he asked, unbelievingly, obviously thinking me a bit of a weed.

Well you know how it is,' I mockingly joked, 'they'll take anyone these days.'

I laughed inside when he replied, not maliciously,

'That's what I thought.'

We all know what thought did, don't we?

To the nicer people amongst us, my attitude and approach to door work is acceptable and respected. That's why I'd never change it and anyway, what's the point of trying to be something you're not? If God wanted to be laid back and cool, like Clint Eastwood, I'd have been born with a cigar in my mouth and six guns by my side, saying to the nurse,

'Are you gonna cut the cord or are you gonna whistle a dixie?'

Another thing I never do is work under the influence of alcohol, though modern misconceptions say all door men do. I allow myself four halves of a lager a night and a packet of crisps please and no more. Any actions or decisions you make in this job should be done soberly, for obvious reasons. Most good fighters only ever lose when they're drunk, which in my eye is no excuse. There is a winner and a loser and that's all the records will show. People always say, he only beat me because I was drunk, but if that's the case, why do they never come back for a straightener when they're sober?

Another thing that always bugs me is when people say the door is easy because you only ever fight kids or drunks and that they are easy pickings. You do fight your fair share of 'kids' and of drunks, but the easy picking bit is a terrible misconception. Most young men who want to fight you are hungry for a reputation and beating a 'named' door man is overnight stardom form them. There is no stronger motivation than this to win. They have fitness and youth on their side and so many these days are into one fighting art or another that young men are potentially very dangerous. As for the drunk, he is the most dangerous and most under estimated fighter on God's earth. Why? Because alcohol makes him completely irrational and any morals he may have held in a sober state will be diluted down or lost with the beer. He will do things, glass or stab you etc that he would never usually dream of. Also, due to the anaesthetising qualities of the old amber nectar, he will often take a lot of 'putting away.' So contrary to popular belief, they are not easy pickings. I under estimate and 'no class' no one. If necessary I will hit them drunk, sober, young or old without any discrimination.

'Granite Jaw' exemplifies the drunk excellently. There are those you can beat by playing scared and there are those you can psych out and back down by playing it fearless. Then there are those who you can do anything with, but fight. Granite Jaw, my hardest ever fight, was one of those. He hung out with the Holbrooks Boys, who, though they carried a fierce fighting reputation, were a nice bunch of lads. Every Friday they drank in the Diplomat and although they never gave us any bother, I always sensed from the attitude of one or two of them that they never rated myself or Kenny 'the body builder.' I knew that sooner or later we were going to have to make our mark with them to establish some respect.

The fight with Granite Jaw was catalysed by this feeling, rather than what he actually said to me on the night. His comments weren't really cause for battle, more the straw that broke the camel's back. Granite wasn't a huge man at 14 stone, but held an inner strength I'd never known in a fighter before or since. His head was sort of square, like a concrete box and his skin slightly pitted. His voice was slow and monotonous with his beige, baggy, cotton shirt hiding the hardened frame of a manual worker. Two of his friends had started fighting and Kenny and I separated them. I started to escort one of them out of the pub when Granite Jaw, in a semi drunken stupor, shouted at me from the podium of a nearby stool to leave his mate alone. I, in no uncertain terms, told him to mind his own fucking business. Having ejected his mate, I came back into the pub, still angry at Granite trying to tell me my job. I pointed my finger at him and using the fearless approach warned him,

'Don't you ever tell me how to do my job.'

It never psyched him out and his return was aggressive.

'I weren't telling you your job.'

I got closer.

'You fucking were. If I want to throw someone out of the pub, I'll do it, so just you mind your own business.'

He was adamant,

'You're out of order. My mate's alright.'

It was an argument I wasn't going to win and his argumentative arrogance was rapidly losing me face. I lined up him up with a right and as soon as he opened his mouth again to speak, 'BANG!'

I let it go. It was right on target. He stumbled off his stool, but to my astonishment, he was still upright and to all intents and purposes unshaken. The shock of this paused me for a second, then I let go with a couple more punches before I was pulled off him.

'What was that for?' he asked, as though all I'd done was slap his face.

Hiding my disbelief, I said,

'Don't you ever try to tell me my job.'

At this, his mates dragged him out of the pub and I was left wondering why I hadn't finished the job properly. A couple of minutes later I looked outside. He was there with his mates, waiting for me. With his left hand he waved me out. Not seeing the point in delaying the inevitable I went outside.

'What did you hit me for?' he asked.

'You know why,' I replied.

'I never done fuck all,' he persisted.

Sensing he was going strike any minute, I lined him up, hiding my preparation with,

'So what are you trying to say,' thinking that maybe he did just want to talk.

I made the mistake of hesitating and not throwing my precooked punch. His right rose to serve me pennants for my mistake, but already lined up, I beat him to the punch.

'BANG!' Right on the button again.

This time he's got to go. He staggered sideways as though falling, then, again to my astonishment, he squared up and came forward. Damn that boy's got a strong jaw! I threw several punches that bounced of his face like flies off a car windscreen. I changed to the body and threw a low roundhouse to his midsection. He came right inside as I recovered it, slowly, I'm afraid, and I felt the backs of my legs against the edge of a four foot by four foot circular, concrete rubbish bin - oh the shame of it! I fell in backwards and was one with yesterday's news and last night's chip packets.

Granite Jaw, all fourteen stone of him, fell on top of me. We both exchanged blows as we struggled to get out. I almost sought sanctuary under an empty crisp packet, but a sleeping wasp had beaten me to it. Granite, being in the inevitable position of 'on top,' managed to get out, but I was still stuck fast. He rained blows and insanities at me whilst his mates cheered him on. Surprisingly, even though at this point I was losing, I never felt any panic. All I needed was a foot hold and this came in the guise of his right index finger. He left it by my mouth a millisecond too long and I snapped it up. He tried to pull his finger free, so I bit it harder. I felt a popping sensation as my teeth severed his skin and the blood oozed from his finger in to my mouth. 'Oh no!' I thought, 'I'm not wearing a condom!' With his bleeding finger right in my mouth I reached out with my right hand and grabbed his testicles. Using them and him, I prised my way out of the bin. I kept biting his finger harder and harder in an attempt at weakening him, so he might give in, but drunkenness and stubbornness made him carry on.

With my left hand I grabbed his cotton shirt to give myself better leverage and some pulling power. I double stepped back and with my right foot, I kicked him straight between the legs. He still wouldn't give in. I was starting to get disheartened. Nothing I hit him with seemed to have any effect.

With his near severed finger still in the grip of my teeth and my left hand still gripping his near ripping shirt tightly, I slightly widened my stance and bit harder on his finger to distract him from what I was about to do. As he yelled in pain I released by bite hold on the finger and pulled him rapidly towards me with both hands. At the same time, thrusting my head forward, I head butted him straight in the face, once, then twice with every ounce of energy and spirit that I could muster. He hit the ground like a concrete pillar and I thought his lights were out. But no, the strong bastard was still conscious and holding on to the shirt that he had ripped off my back as he fell.

'All right, all right,' he yelled, 'I've had enough.'

As the words left his lips, I lifted my right foot in the air and stamped on his face. There was no way I was going to let this man get back up. At this stage his mates, seeing that he was losing, rushed towards me only to be yanked back by my ginger haired 'pocket Hercules' friend Kenny the bodybuilder, who'd grabbed the leather sleeves of their jackets, ripping them off in the process. My second stamp was cut short by the arrival of the Boys in Blue. I disappeared into the crowd of spectators that had gathered and then hid in the pub toilets. Kenny held the fort outside.

A couple of weeks later, Granite came to see me at the pub to apologise. I shook his hand and later we became good friends. I will always respect him for being such a tough opponent, but more so for being man enough to shake my hand afterwards.

The 'Canly' boys were also tough, but that's all the praise they'll get from me. They were all servants of the 'Dark Side.' The life savers they carried though, came in the guise of 'Pils' bottles.

Monday night, 10:30. The venue, the Wyken Pippin. Mondays were always quiet and this one seemed quieter than most. My eyes were half closed. Sleep was calling me.

'CRASH!'

I awoke to the sight and sound of five or six fighting youths. 'Oh no! Young and drunk!' Tony 'the head' and I ran to the disturbance. One lad was unconscious by the bar, his head split like a melon by a flailing Pils bottle. Crimson adorned his face and head and another two were fighting on the floor. One sat on top of the other, playing the drums on his face with two Pils bottles - nice boy. I dragged him off using a left hand rear choke, my right hand around his arm and body in an attempt at trying to stop him from hitting me with the bottles. Mr Ungrateful on floor, whose life I had just saved, started kicking me in the legs for my troubles, so I showed his chin a short round house and he was sleeping. Whilst I tightened my choke on Mr Pils, Tony dragged another pair out of the pub. The fact Mr Pils wouldn't release the bottles from his grip wasn't too bad, but the fact that he was trying to hit me in the face with them was really starting to piss me off.

'Drop the bottles!' I told him, through gritted, angry teeth.

'When I get out of this I'm going to fucking kill you,' he replied, in an angry, choking whisper.

My lock was obviously taking its toll on the poor fellow. I could tell he didn't like me and that he meant what he said, but he wasn't really in a very good position to be calling the odds. I tightened my lock to just less than knock out pressure. His breathing was shallow and almost non-existent.

'Drop the bottles!' I said again.

This time he dropped them like hot coals. I released the hold I had on him and as he turned around I fired a short right hook at his jaw and he went the same way as the bottles. As he landed, I heaved an axe kick into his ribs and left him for dead. Mr Ungrateful was just coming around from his short, unexpected trip to sleepsville, so I thought I'd just show him the way out. As I leaned over to pick him up, I felt the wind of a punch on the back of my head. How it missed me, I'll never know. I instinctively turned and ran at my would be attacker with a blitz of punches. I grabbed him by the shoulders and rammed him face first into the brick pillar by the edge of the dance floor. His nose smashed on impact. As he turned around, I put all my weight behind a right cross that sent him toppling to the carpet. I was so incensed at his attempt at 'Judasing' me, that I dropped the axe kick into his ribs. He let out a low pitiful moan, as though all the life had just left his body. I turned just in time to see Tony head-butting another baddie into the fruit machine.

Between us, Tony and I carried what was left of the Pils Brigade out onto the car park. They lay scattered on the ground, like bomb victims. We went back into the club thinking that was the end of it all. We were silently pleased with a job well done - brutally, I grant you, but you can only fight fire with fire.

We were just about to enjoy a well earned drink, when 'CRASH!', then 'CRASH!' again and the windows started going in. They were outside, with an new lease of life, smashing windows and calling Tony and I outside. We went straight out. They were only three now, but my goodness, they were angry and a little battered too. I walked towards the first one, Tony towards the second. Mine cursed and spat at me as I approached. I walked slowly and predictably, ignoring the spit that hit and passed me. I was only looking at his feet, lining him up with a sweep. He was too blind with anger and venom to notice this. His lips were still puckering from the third spit and the spit missiling through the air as I rushed in and executed a vicious back leg sweep - my speciality at the time. It would have toppled a grizzly! His elbow gave out a loud cracking sound as he landed on it and his head thwacked the gravel, leaving little bits of stone embedded into his scalp. He was asleep. Tony's mate pulled out a knife, but a little too slowly, so Tony bounced a chair leg off his head.

Now it was a race for the third, who was still cursing obscenities at us. A bit silly really, considering that he was now alone. I, being a little fitter than Tony, reached him first and spent little energy in putting him away. As we entered the door of the pub, they were starting to recover and began to shout threats at us once again. I suppressed a yawn. I'd heard it all a hundred times before and needless to say, these threats were never realised either.

Mr C was/is a well known fighter, come villain in the city of Coventry. But, I'm afraid for a supposedly learned man, he hadn't learned a lot. Had he, he might have realised that although my book cover may resemble that of a love story or a book of poems, it is in fact concealing the text of a potentially violent, veteran street fighter.

Mr C was a hard faced, mean looking man, in his early forties, with a beard and multiple scars, from past wars, on his face. His eyes were squinty and crazy with a turned up dwarf nose. His permanently frowning face never shared a smile and he'd done much time for his quickness with a puncturing tool. He'd also ran riot on more than one occasion, with a 'sawn off.' He was psychotic and definitely 'plastic.'

The Navigation was a knife's throw from Bell Green, home of the infamous 'Crew' and sat detached at the foot of a hump back bridge, backing onto Coventry canal. This had always been a rough pub with much violence most weekend nights. Recent refurbishment called for new doormen to put an end to the said violence. My name was mentioned, good money was offered, so here I was.

The new system, refurbishment, and new doormen was working well. The pub was attracting nice people who wanted only a good fun night out, without trouble. We had expected a visit from the 'Bell Green Crew' - the rumour was that they resented me working their patch and were going to send down a reception committee to welcome me, as it were. But the said visit was not forthcoming and everything on the Western front was clear. At least it was until we were honoured by the Mr C visit.

He entered the lounge of the 'Navvy' with about six of his cronies. As he entered, everything but the music stopped or at least it seemed to. Everyone in the busy lounge knew who and what he was. They ambled over to the bar and Mr C stood with his back to the bar, scanning the whole room. This was his kingdom and nobody fixed his stare, they all just turned away. Eye contact with this man was enough and had been enough in the past to put a knife in you, so it was best avoided. Within about ten minutes of him being there, several people, all independent of each other approached me with,

'Do you know who that is?' or 'Geoff, Mr C's in.'

Mr B, his tall, heavy set, short haired, dopey faced companion (a money lender with a habit of breaking legs) was by Mr C's side. Between them they held the district in a grip of fear that few seemed to be able to break. Mr C's estranged wife was also in the pub tonight and he was not happy about it. Right from the minute they walked in, I knew there was going to be trouble. My sixth sense for violence was born to years of dealing with it and violent people. I'd learnt to almost smell it and tonight the air was thick with its repugnance. The first thing I did was to go to the toilet and empty my bladder. Crude I know, but it's a habit many fighters acquire. Then I tightened my shoe laces and I was ready.

I sat talking to Gill, one of our off duty bar maids. I didn't know it at the time, but she was sat with the blonde, pretty ex-wife of Mr C. I didn't know her from Adam, but I guess the jealous ex thought that I did and even if I didn't, it was his excuse to let me know who he was and not to fuck with him. He walked towards me.

'Alright Paul,' I said politely.

He crashed through my courtesy,

'Can I have a word with you outside?'

My adrenal gland flushed some liquid dynamite into my blood stream - 'Here we go' I thought. Outside we squared off. Mr B, his henchman, shadowed his rear and I kept a suspicious eye on the beer glass in C's right hand. I didn't want to be wearing it, it just wasn't my colour.

'I don't want to row with you,' he said, 'but I'm not happy about what's going on in there tonight, so I'm just telling you, keep your neck out.'

You're confused? How do you think I felt? I didn't have a clue what the maniac was going on about.

'I'm not being funny mate, but I don't know what you're talking about.'

I was just being honest, as I didn't. He looked at Mr B for guidance, but he was a few cells short of a full brain and just shrugged his shoulders. He looked back at me and pointed.

'I'm just telling you to keep your neck out.'

I shrugged and looked at them both, trying not to sound scared.

'Seriously, I don't know what you mean. You'll have to explain because I'm in the dark.'

He conceded.

'My missus is in there and I don't like it, so I'm just letting you know the score.'

'Is she the blonde one?' I asked.

'Yeah,' he replied.

'That's fair enough,' I said, already realising that he'd overstepped the mark.

We walked back in to the glare of many eyes. They all knew what was going on. I took stock of the situation and analysed what he had said to me. As I sat thinking, I watched Mr C approach the pub manager menacingly.

'Get everyone out of the pub,' he growled, his face almost touching the manager's. 'Or I'm going to fucking wreck the place.'

He obviously thought he'd backed me down outside and that I wasn't in the frame any longer or he wouldn't be talking to the manager like he was. He didn't know me very well.

After a short analysis, I came to the conclusion that Mr C had in no uncertain terms warned me off in my own gaff. This I couldn't live with. I'd rather be beaten to a pulp than bottle out. The day I let anyone bully me again is the day I give up living. I approached Tony and told him what had been said.

'I can't live with it Tony, I'm going to give him a square go. Will you watch my back?'

Tony's eyes looked scared and his hand shook as he lifted his cigarette to his mouth. He nodded his consent. I knew that he wasn't scared, it was just the demon adrenalin running through his veins. I took off my bow tie and Tony and I approached Mr C and his mates.

'Can I have a word with you outside?' I asked him.

Now it was my turn. As I spoke, everybody turned and stared. Mr C's reply was blunt and confident,

'If you want to talk, come do it here.'

'Alright. I don't know you and I don't know your missus. You come in here, where I'm the head doorman and insult. I can't live with it,' I said, then I looked at his mates and back at him again.

'No disrespect to your mates, but we're going to have to have a fight. A one on one. Me and you in the car park. No seconds, just you and me.'

I watched, amazed as his spirit left him. He never expected this and stuttered as he spoke.

'Hold on a minute. You misunderstood me. I didn't mean to insult you.'

I couldn't believe what I was hearing. The fortress that stood before me was obviously built on very shaky foundations. I never would have believed that a man on such a high pedestal would be so easily toppled, but not one to look a gift horse in the mouth.

'Well, I took it as an insult, so all I'm saying is we'll have a square go.'

He bought it again.

'I never meant it as an insult, you misunderstood me.'

'Alright, we'll leave it at that then,' I concluded.

I walked away, ten feet tall. Tony grabbed my face and kissed my forehead.

'That was brilliant Geoff, I'm proud of you,' he said.

I smiled at his compliment. If I thought that that was the end of it though, I was gravely mistaken. It was nearly the end of the night anyway, so most of the people who hadn't left were about to leave. Soon there were only the staff, a few friends and the 'enemy' left. Mr C had lost face badly, so something had to happen. It did. Mr B, the brain shy one, left the pub only to return seconds later with a base ball bat that might have seconded for a lamppost. My adrenalin hit red alert, but I managed to hide it and control it, ready for the harness. Mr C walked away from the bar and looked over at me.

'You, outside!' he shouted, pointing at me.

'Right,' I accepted, glad that it was nearly over. I rolled my sleeves up and followed him out. Inside Tony stood off his stool. Mr B, bat in hand, shook his head.

'One on one,' he said

Tony nodded and sat back down. Outside, I squared up to Mr C, who realising that he'd obviously got a fight on his hands, back peddled.

'I don't want to fight with you, man.'

He walked towards me with his right hand extended in a friendly gesture. Was he scared or just playing scared to get a shot at me? I took no chances and pushed him back.

'Stay where you are!' I warned. He smiled.

'I can see you're wary of me, but I don't want to row with you. It's a misunderstanding, you misunderstood what I said.'

Again he offered to shake hands. I took the chance and shook his hand warily. Mr B came out of the pub, bat at the ready. I could see he was on edge, hiding his build up badly. 'I'll remember that chink in your armour for the next time' I thought.

'Everything sorted then?' he asked Mr C.

'Yeah, it's resolved,' he said.

It's because he backed down, that's why, but I don't suppose he'll tell his mates that. But I know and he knows and that's good enough for me.

Chapter 10

David and Goliath

A fifteen year old delinquent Mike Tyson, carrying the beginnings of frame that would one day make him the idol of millions, looked in awed admiration at the peak bulging sinewy biceps of a Cus Damatio fighter. Cus, the aging, tiny boxing trainer of many champions noticed the impressionable Tyson's envious gaze and shook his head knowingly.

'No Mike,' he said, tapping his right index finger against his temple.

'This is where big is.'

'B' was the biggest thing that ever squeezed through the double doors of the Walsgrave club, his six feet two frame struggling to hold the 22 stone of fat that hung from it. He was much disliked in this newly multi roomed, one levelled abode where the working men and women and the area drank and married. He was also much feared so few dared tell him of their dislike. I'd personally witnessed his destruction of many name fighters before me, he was especially known for biting off anything that stuck out, dangled or protruded the surface of his opponents body, especially noses: he liked noses.

He was a bully, and the dark side was his battering ram. He was a big chap, no matter where you sat in a room, the 'B' sat next to you.

A bright, early Saturday July evening saw me through the doors of the club that lay neatly between the two modern housing estates in Walsgrave. A nicer part of the city, where the cancerous shadow of violence had not completely darkened. My four 'weekend' children and I trod the spongy soft carpeted entrance, by-passed the concert room, and entered the small games room through the large table-and-chaired bar that lay empty and motionless, awaiting the evening rush.

My wife and I were divorced, the weekend was my chance to top up the children's love that I so badly missed. Next time anyone tells you that a kick between the legs from a bucking horse is the most painful thing known to Man, laugh at them. Divorce is far more painful.

My three girls ranged between twelve and seven and inherited my damn good looks, my little boy was one and half at the time, he was a proper little chap and followed me everywhere. Saturday at the club was their weekly treat.

The bar, a two tabled snooker room and bagatel room, was divided only by a glass partition that was based by a run of red leather-look seating that overlooked the snooker tables on the one side and the bar on the other. We sat in the bagatel room, in a little nook to the right of the snooker tables. The kids were throwing plastic flighted darts at the dart board and drawing chalk pictures on the score board, I was enjoying the solitude of a near empty room.

My amblings over things, past, present and to come were shattered by the ear piercing crash of a glass ash tray as it met its end on the bar floor. I turned to see the retracting hand of the 'B' who was sat with his back to me at the end of the partition seats just inside the bar. I watched in disgust as he 'frisbeed' another ash tray across the bar. The eyes of the few that were in there were all on him, but they kept their distance and were careful not to let him see they were looking. He was feared and a he knew it. A part of me wanted to go over and sort him out, but another part of me said 'no', it was none of my business. But who was going to stop him? Most of the committee men were old and those who were not old were rightly scared. This man was an animal, he was like a fox in a chicken run.

I'd got enough trouble in my life then without inviting in another 22 stones worth, no, I decided to leave him to his own devices. Maybe we would be lucky and he'd become Walsgrave's first case of spontaneous combustion. He certainly had enough fat to fuel the fire. I sat back on my morals and watched with everyone else as he smashed the place up. Then he made a mistake, a big mistake. He blindly skimmed a tin ash tray behind him and at great speed it passed by me, my eyes followed its flight and descent with almost helpless agony as it spun like a flying saucer towards my little boy's head. I closed my eyes in relief as it narrowly missed him and clattered to the floor. My ears reopened their channels and I was out of chair and over to the 'B' before the ash tray had stopped gyrating on the floor.

'Someone catch that did they?' he scoffed without even looking up at me. His face, that seemed wider than the diameter of his skull stared forward, not even affording me the courtesy of a look. All my self control had gone, my short fuse was burnt out and I exploded.

'You fat bastard, if you ever do that again I'm gonna fucking kill you.' I'd always been good with words. He turned, visually unperturbed by my verbal onslaught, then he began to rise and his shadow engulfed me. I wondered if this was a total eclipse of the sun.

'Is that right?' he replied, coolly. In my blind rage I'd forgotten to position myself properly, I was square on with no time to line him up, so I hit him with a half cocked left hook, my right redundant with a wrist fracture. It wasn't my best shot but it was good enough, his many chins shook and wobbled upon contact and he fell back in his seat like a beached whale. I was all over him like a rash, raining in several left hand punches to his face, the table in front of him protecting him from any attempt at kicks. As three of the locals pulled me off him I shouted and cursed more abuse his way, my temper still in control. He stood up, massaging his jaw, looking shaken.

'If I was out of order I apologise,' he said, offering me his left hand to shake. I was suspicious, I had an idea what he was up to. His usual trick was to offer the hand as bait, and when you took it he would yank you into a 22 stone headbutt. I reluctantly took a chance and extended my hand.

As soon as he gripped it I felt the beginnings of a pull.

'Get the fuck off me,' I said.

'Anytime you want to tread the pavement with me just let me know.'

'Anytime,' I underlined. Just as I said this one of his followers whispered in his ear.

"B', that's Geoff Thompson, he's a doorman.'

'B' sat down immediately on hearing this. As I gathered my kids together to leave, Kerry my oldest girl was shaking.

'You alright?' I asked

'Yeah,' she said, then, 'Dad, when he stood up he was massive, you looked dead tiny.' I laughed,

'He didn't stay up for long though did he?'

Apparently, shortly after I left so did the 'B'. Whilst I was at home sipping a hot cup of tea he was down another pub biting the nose of a cowering youth in retribution for the 'slap' that I gave him.

Two weeks later I arrived at work at the 'Devon' with Sharon by my side to find the 'B' waiting for me.

'Is that Geoff Thompson?' he asked my friend Kenny 'the body builder'.

'Yes, that's him,' came the reply. He walked towards me and I automatically lined him up, but there was no need to. He was meek.

'I think I owe you an apology, don't I?'

I was cold. 'Yes you do.'

'Was I out of order?' he asked.

'Yeah,' I replied. He shot his right hand out pathetically towards me, gesturing that we shake hands.

'I'm really sorry, I was drunk, the lads spiked my drink, please take my hand on it.' I shook his hand. I admired him for apologising, that takes a big man, and he was definitely a big man.

Owen stood five feet six and weighed in at, if I exaggerate, nine and a half stone. He is about 20 years old, but looks five years younger. He's the man on the beach that you just love to kick sand at with his waif-like physique and cheeky grin, he is the proverbial swat from 'Tom Brown's' school days. However his hands are perfectly formed tools for the trade of boxing, they rata-tat-tat on the punch bag like bullets from an Uzi. His footwork is smooth and precise, reflecting the pro boxer he is, but he's not just a ring technician, this man can do it for real. So many fighters leave their ability in the gym, but not Owen. He's put his hands on more opponents in live situations than I care to or have time to tell you about and I love him. He has more balls than a Japanese ping-pong team and he very rarely goes out without getting involved in some kind of altercation. Basically, I believe the reason for this is that he looks so inoffensive and that he is cheeky. He won't take any stick off anyone. When people have a go at him he retaliates and they think it's their birthday.

'Squeeze me, love,' they tell their ladies, 'I'm just going to teach this boy some manners.' Their consciousness and pride is brutally taken away from them as he explodes in a torrent of torturous techniques. When someone hits you with nine stone, believe me, it's like being hit with a hammer. He's like a ferret on a mission.

The 'Dip' sets the scene for his bout with 'Goliath'. A small pub on the edge of the city centre, secluded behind two trees growing through the pavement, it was once known for the violence it spewed out every, and I mean every, weekend. Nowadays it was known as a warm, busy, friendly pub, meticulously straightened-out by 'Cash' who forged his standards with an iron will and high-quality doormen. A small room with soft-seat edging, dance floor and bar was divided by an old brick fireplace in the middle of the room. Some said that it took up too much space but I thought it gave the place warmth. Pictures of the local football team and Karate men adorned the wall above the bar which curved around to Cash's Cocktail Bar. The cocktail craze however, lasted little longer than Coventry's football success.

Owen hated Joe who was a doorman from 'The Lane'. His name as a doorman was nearly as bad as his breath: another bully with respect for little or nothing. He stood at least six feet four tall and eighteen stone with a shirt button popping beer-belly, trousers which shone with the thousands of ironings they had been subjected to and scuffed, scruffy half-polished shoes - smart for the building site, maybe, but not for here. His hair was side-parted and greased, his face permanently wearing a five o'clock shadow - young but aged with beer, smoke and late nights. He was with his lady who looked rougher than a piece of sandpaper but by hi standards she was good. He was out to impress.

Owen and Joe's eyes met across a crowded room. Violence was on the menu. Joe's lady noticed this straight away as he stopped talking to her and turned away, oblivious to her and everyone else around. Owen felt the fire of fear ignite in his stomach as Joe approached. The doorman, warned by a sixth sense born to the job, homed in on the scene. As the two met, a circle formed around them, broken only by the doormen. Joe poked Owen aggressively,

'You! I'll have you anytime!' His face grimaced with hatred. Owen was too small and knew that Joe could take him. His face broke into a nervous grin as he realised what Joe was thinking.

'Come into my parlour said the spider to the fly.'

'Outside now then,' Owen retorted. Joe turned to his lady and removed the cheap watch from his wrist that wasn't even worth breaking, but that was not why he removed it. It was the same as taking off your jacket and rolling up your sleeves before battle. It's a fighter's last ditch attempt at scaring his opponent but this time it wasn't going to work. The doormen never intervened, never even spoke; there was no need. It was the courtesy that they afforded fighters who had enough respect to take their arguments off the premises. Owen walked outside. Joe was heard to whisper to his lady,

'This won't take long.' He was right - it wouldn't. He was about to be beaten a lot quicker than he thought. The chip shop across the road emptied as it did every time there was a fight outside in the street. The Parson's Nose was where everybody went for supper after the pubs and night clubs closed. More than just fish got battered at this chippy. The food there was great but not as good as the entertainment. The two squared up, Owen opting for the traditional boxing stance, Joe for the 'I don't know what the fuck I'm doing - I just rely on my size' stance. Fists were clenched at waist level. Joe towered over Owen and, to the uninitiated, it looked like this would be a slaughter. Owen skipped around, sizing up his man. Joe bludgeoned forward with the grace of an ox. Owen retreated slightly, caught his heel on a bit of protruding slab (fucking council) and fell to the ground. Joe's eyes lit up as if to say 'Oh great!'. Owen winced as if to say 'Oh shit!'. But before Joe could take advantage of this error, sprightly Owen sprang back to his feet, guard high, dancing around this oak tree of a man with an acorn for a brain. Joe pursed his lips angrily - he'd had enough and was about to swat this irritating firefly. He rushed in. Bang! 'Where did that come from?' his expression seemed to cry as he entered Owen's space and the knuckles of a left hook connected with his jaw. 'We don't know,' replied his legs, 'but we're going down.' The oak tree was felled. Owen rushed in using Joe's head as a football. Joe was finished. The doormen pulled Owen away just as the police appeared on the scene and Owen made his getaway.

Kerry is very slight, just a wisp of a girl. Long dark hair, brown eyes and a lovely little upturned nose like a little pixie. Very pretty but very modest. As small as an eleven year old but as mature as fifteen. At thirteen she's quite a little lady. She has mood swings that are relative and usual for her age but she has a good heart and a lovely nature. I've met a lot of strong people in my life, many braver than their ability but none do I admire for spirit as I do her. She's only a baby and yet she has so much to learn but I don't want to impose too much knowledge of fighting on one so young.

Should I teach her choking techniques, line-ups, biting? Should I teach my baby dirty fighting? Many would say that it is morally wrong, but is it? I've heard of girls a lot younger than her being beaten up or raped. The lads at school would hit a girl as quick as, if not quicker than another lad. At three years of age, I started my little girl in my own Karate class so she could grow up with it and be part of it. At the age of eleven, she attained her black belt, first dan under the Japanese. At eleven she also started at Cardinal Wiseman secondary school and passed down the very same corridors in which I had cried tears of disdain, the very same playground that held haunting memories of my bullied youth and she would attend the very same chapel where I knelt on wooden kneeling benches in the chill of stone prison like walls.

The chapel in which I clasped my hands together in prayer that these feelings would go away, that I would suddenly emerge from this holy place surrounded by heavenly light, transformed into a brave little boy who would no longer be picked on, who would be able to go home at night and eat a dinner that, for once, would enter a stomach that was not churning with grief. I wished that I could sleep a peaceful sleep and awaken to the sun shining and the birds singing, not to a cold, dark, drizzly morning that dared me to confront the day, dared me, in fact, to confront life.

Would I ever again be able to kiss the warm lips and hold the soft hand of Kim Clancy without worrying about whether or not Robert-The Fat Bastard-Best was going to pick on me again the next day? I worried about whether Kerry would to be forced to endure what I was. My mind wandered back five years to Karate class in the cold, wooden-floored skating rink. The hall was so cold that Kerry's little six year old pixie nose was blue as she shivered and a tear welled up in her eye and rolled down her cheek. I looked at her and nearly cried myself. I cuddled her and told her to go and get changed. She shook her head and said that she wanted to carry on.

Mary was two years older than Kerry and twice the size of her. Too big for Kerry. She was a nice girl really but she had it in for my girl and always picked on her in the Karate class. I'd never really picked up on it before because Mary would never do it when I was around and Kerry was too proud to tell me. I heard the dull thud of a chest punch with a little suppressed whimper on the end of it. I turned to see Kerry and Mary sparring, both were brown belts now but Kerry was still too small for Mary. Thud again. Everybody else was sparring so no-one noticed this but me. Kerry tried to fight back but Mary's whole being seemed to envelop her. Tears welled up in Kerry's eyes and ran down her face as they fought. I wanted to pull her out, to free her and to take away her pain but I knew I couldn't. She had to fight it and control it herself. I offered her words of encouragement as they fought but to no avail. It was hurting me to watch: my heart was aching.

'Stop!' I shouted. I could bear no more. 'Kerry, do you want to stop and have a rest?' I was giving her a loop-hole, a way out and I could see that she wanted to take it. She was desperate to take it. She shook her head.

'Are you sure?' I gave her one more chance. She nodded, too choked to talk. I was so proud of her. She was too young to realise then but these victories over yourself are the absolute foundation upon which character building is based. As fate would have it, another girl joined the club shortly after this incident who was more Mary's size so I partnered those two. With no malice, this girl gave to Mary for one entire lesson, what Kerry had endured for two years. I saw in Mary's face what I had seen in Kerry's. Mary left my club after that lesson and never trained with me again. What goes around comes around.

The frame of Kerry's maths room door was worn and ragged and the quarry tiled floor on which she stood held no warmth. Neither for that matter did a double period of maths but when you're thirteen and just part of your way through education, it is just one of the things that you have to endure. This she could bear. What she found absolutely intolerable was this snotty-nosed, scruffy, ignorant kid in front of her who kept pushing and poking her. It was probably something as simple as him fancying her and this was his way of showing her. She held herself back for a bit, trying to avoid any conflict but in the end it all got too much.

'Will you stop flipping poking me,' she angrily shouted. His reply was to grab her hair and to call her an unrepeatable name. As he pulled her hair a little harder and turned her body to the left, she gritted her teeth, moved her left leg to form a forty-five degree stance and put a right hand reverse punch, smack between the egg-stained lapels of his black blazer, right on the solar plexus. He hit the ground and skidded on his backside along the tiled floor. Shock adorned his face, then he frantically grabbed the air as though to replace the lot that Kerry had just knocked out of him. Everyone looked in amazement as he gasped for air, none more amazed than Kerry who was carefully examining her right hand. 'Did I really do that?' she seemed to ask herself. The winded one never had to ask that though. He knew.

Chapter 11

Humour In adversity: bomb at the Pippin

The tall, dark, wood stool, with green velvet seat, sat me by the customary wooden bar while I savoured the smooth, oh so tasty bottle of Budweiser and crunched away at the smoky bacon crisps that were more inviting that an coal fire on a winter's night. It was 8:30 p.m., the start of my shift. It should have started at eight, but being late had always been a doorman's privilege.

Another quiet week day night with only the die hard locals at home. Most of them were in the pool room, around the corner of the lounge and to the left. I felt the cold autumn breeze on the back of my neck as the entrance door behind me fell open. I turned my head to see what the said breeze had blown in. He was average in height and carried what I perceived to be a sombre, callous look under the untidiness of his long, dark hair that over shadowed his lengthy, beige, dirty detective-cum-terrorist type mac that even Columbo would have binned - yes, it was a scruffy coat. Casually draped over his left shoulder was a graffitied canvas rucksack, you know, the type one might conceal a bomb in. He stopped just inside the door and ran his eyes around the entirety of the room, stopping briefly as they met with mine. His scanning of the joint told me that he was indeed a very suspicious specimen. His scruffy, mud stained plimsoll pumps carried him across the room, down the carpeted steps and around the corner towards the pool room, out of my sight. I analysed the situation and came to the conclusion that my fears and suspicions were born mainly to paranoia. There had been a spate of bomb scares in the city recently and bombing in the news had been the norm. I guess they had stuck in my mind to such an extent that I was becoming suspicious of every columbo mac'd, steely eyed, bomb carrying terrorist type that happened to pass by.

'I'll just finish this bottle of Bud and these delicious smokey bacon crisps and I'll check him out,' I told myself. But before I could get crisp to mouth, my terrorist friend was making his exit. His slow, predictable pace was now erased by a worried hurried kind of walk. My ears pricked up like an alerted Alsatian. 'Well, at least he's gone,' I told myself. My relief at his exit was short lived though. As he hastily left I noticed that something was missing, the bomb, I mean his rucksack.

'Excuse me sir,' I wanted to shout, 'you've left without your bomb.' But alas, he was gone with the wind, if you'll forgive the pun. I rushed around to the pool room, my eyes searching every nook and cranny en route. Then, there it was, as large and as proud as life, sat to the right of the cowboy type louvre doors that bid entrance to the pool room. 'Ha!' it seemed to goad me, 'What are you gonna do now then?' I really couldn't believe what was happening. Did this canvas really conceal a life threatening device? What should I do? Oh, what a dilemma!

As I got closer to the rucksack it suddenly occurred to me that if this was a bomb, the bloody thing could go off and my dashing good looks would be as one with the decor. Usually in dangerous situations I'd fight to hold on to my bottle. This time I was fighting to hold my bowels. My goodness, this was so real, what about my family? What about my friends and children? What about life itself? It could all be lost to this canvas death sentence that lay ominously before me. I had to do something. It was my job to protect the punters. Yes, but what if I evacuate them all and it's a hoax? Oh, the embarrassment! On the other hand, if it is a bomb and I don't evacuate them, they will all be pebble dashed up the walls as well. I had to be sure, so I got down on my hands and knees and lent my ear to the canvas.

'Oh my goodness, it was ticking!' My stomach turned upside down and then around. Now I had no choice. I had to get everyone out of the building, or at least the pool room. I tried to remain calm. I 'John Wayned' through the louvre doors in to the parlour type pool room where eight played the four tables and in my most authoritative voice said,

'You'll all have to leave the pub.'

Everybody laughed at what they thought was my attempt at a wheeze. I tried again,

'I'm serious. There's a bomb in the place.'

Humour left their faces, not as quick though as they left the pub. I'll have to remember this ploy next time they're a little slow drinking up at the end of the night. Pool cues clattered on to the deserted table greens and with the pool room empty, I returned to my friend the bomb. Looking back, I guess I was pretty stupid, because I got back on my hands and knees by the rucksack to reaffirm that it was a bomb and not just my imagination. Sure enough I was right, it was still ticking.

The sound of footsteps caused me to look up from this very undignified 'doggie position' to see my terrorist friend returning. He gazed down at me with a very bemused look on his face.

'What was I doing,' he wondered to himself, 'listening to his sandwiches?' I watched as the killer terrorist's steely gaze transformed in to the bewildered look of a baby faced student who'd only popped in to the pub for a moment after college to see a friend and in his rush, had left his rucksacked sandwich box.

To add to my embarrassment, the pub manager appeared while I was still on my knees to see why everyone had just vacated his pub. 'Why are you kneeling down in front of this man's rucksack?' he must have thought.

'Can I have my sandwiches back please?' asked the student.

If you don't get out of my face, you'll be wearing them, I wanted to say as I handed him the rucksack. I could have throttled him. The manager failed to suppress an ear to ear grin as I told him my story and I spent the rest of the night trying to avoid the 'evacuees.'

Had it been a bomb and not a 'ticking' sandwich, I might have been a hero, but it wasn't, so I wasn't.

The middle finger of my right hand had swelled up like a fat pork sausage and was beginning to get too stiff to bend. The swelling was also starting to spread in to my hand. It must have been bad, because my cast iron made to measure steel fist would no longer slip over my fingers. I'd cut it the week before, relieving a bully of his front teeth, fragments of which I had to tweezer out of the wound.

I was, to be honest, a bit frightened of hospitals, though I'm not sure why. Well, I am really. It's because you read all these stories in the paper about people going in for trivial things, like my poor finger and coming out with catastrophic, never before heard of diseases or having bits removed in surgery that shouldn't really have been removed - basically I was scared shitless.

After a week though, it should have healed, especially when you consider that I'd virtually emptied the chemist on it, trying to do my Doctor Geoff impersonation. The hospital wasn't what I wanted, but it was what I needed. Anyway, I consoled myself that they'll only give me a tetanus and I'll be away, in and out in an hour. I sat in the magnolia painted, soft beige floor, tiled waiting room of Coventry and Warwickshire Hospital, waiting for my turn to see the doctor. After an hour the hard, wooden bench was beginning to take its toll on my bum.

'Geoffrey Thompson, cubicle two please,' said a faceless voice over the intercom.

I made my way to the cubicle. I felt a little scared. What if they discovered a cancerous growth, or the chap I'd hit had AIDS on the teeth. I wasn't wearing a condom when I punched him, oh no. The doctor was foreign. In 28 years of coming in and out of this hospital, I'd never seen an English doctor. I don't know why that is, though it mattered not. He was polite and articulate,

'You have an abscess, we're going to have to admit you.'

My adrenalin ran riot as my worst fears were realised. 'Oh shit, this is it.' Philip ward looked old and absolutely Victorian, though spotlessly clean, with a smell that only a hospital could emit. It always reminded me of death. Every bed I passed down the corridor-like ward seemed to hold someone either really ill or really old and although the nurses here were thanklessly brilliant at their jobs and in their kindness, I couldn't help thinking what a horrible place it would be to spend your last dying days. My bed was a duplicate of every hospital bed I'd ever slept in. Neat as a pin and hard as a nail. It was like sleeping on a bed on concrete with paper sheets that seemed glued to the foot of the bed when, in the middle of the cold night, you tried to pull them over you. I asked the nurse if I could use the toilet before I got changed.

'Of course,' she said, 'but take this bottle with you. We want a sample.'

'Why? What has urine got to do with my bloody finger?' Everything that day that had left my body, they wanted a sample of. In the end I was too scared to speak in case they wanted to test that as well.

They had decided to operate that night and probably release me the next day. Was I in prison? The operation to remove an abscess from my 'tooth decayed' finger went smoothly and I thought my problems were over - yippee, home today! Then I saw them, the student nurses following from bed to bed the surgeon of the ward.

'This is Mr Smith,' I could hear them say in the next row of beds to mine. 'He fell off a ladder and broke his right hip. We have to replace it with a plastic hip,' etc, etc.

'Oh No! This could be embarrassing. I wanted to hide, to crawl away. I hoped the room would open up and swallow me. I pulled the blankets around me, covering my head in the hope that they might not see me, like the proverbial Ostrich. I was still hiding, but could hear their feet coming towards my bed, could feel their condemning eyes and hear their light banter.

'This is Mr Thompson,' he said.

I peeped over the top of my blankets. He paused a second, looking back at my notes, then again at me.

'He has an abscess in the middle finger of his right hand, caused by punching somebody in the teeth.'

He held his stare, then moved to the next bed, followed by the giggling student nurses. The last of the bunch turned to me and whispered,

'Did you knock him out?'

I nodded.

'Good,' she said.

The rain fell with increasing ease, the melodious pitter patter on the tarmacked car park was lullabying me into sleepsville. 10:55 and counting. Five long minutes to closing. Time distortion was boxing the head off me. Monday nights were always quiet and this Monday proved no exception. The mobile chip van parked on the roadside at the edge of the pub car park and waited in anticipation. Thye diet taunting smell that yelled out at you, 'cholesterol,

cholesterol' drfited into the pub and lingered in the air, teasing, tempting and drawing out the drinkers like rats to the piper.

First out were two local, off duty doormen, who fitted into the 'rat' category admirably. 'T' was 6ft tall with a cap of light hair and hungry for trouble look. 'D' stood smaller, but a stone heavier though, at fourteen stone and his sunken, cloud grey, seemingly pupiless eyes were hidden under his high chiseled cheek bones. With a permanent 'Cagney grin,' his quasi hunched shoulders held dangly arms with digger bucket hands. They laughed and joked on exit. Shortly behind them were the 'dummy' twins, two young lads who could have seconded for Pinochio with glared red cheeks and 'nob of wood' noses. They stringed their way out, both carrying a daft pissed smile on their young faces. If they weighed ten stone between them, soaking wet with their clothes under their arms, then that's as much as they did weigh.

T and D stood by the blue bricked steps of the Pippin front door, tucking into their trayed curry and chips. The Pinochio twins staggered over - the steps would make a nice place to capture their balance enough to eat their hot dogs. Eating and walking at the same time, whilst pissed, placed too great a stress on their brains. Alignment between hot dog and mouth was causing great problems. Tony 'the head' and I had just seen the last punter off the premises and were about to leave for home ourselves. We watched and giggled as Pinochio number one's right elbow clipped the base of T's half filled curry tray, knocking it to the floor. T's chip skewered wooden fork froze, suspended by his own agape mouth. They both stared down at the curried tarmac. Pinochio apologised profusely, begging the forgiveness of old 'curryless,' but the hungry one was not amused.

We watched with interest as 'T' grabbed Pinochio's unstarted hot dog from his hand and in pure slapstick fashion, thrust it into his face, then screwing it hard from left to right. Hot dog face shrugged his shoulders in expectance of his penance. Pinochio number two intervened, apologising on his friend's behalf, getting a hard stare off 'T' as his reply. Sensing the lack of forgiveness in the air, the twins decided to go whilst the going was still good, making their way zig zagedly across the car park, over the wall and across the road. They'd got as far as the small row of shops by the time Tony and I had reached my car to the right of the car park. The key was in the driver's door when I noticed T and D pointing and whispering at and about the twins. I knew what they were up to. These two easy targets were far too good to miss up. They ran across the road shouting abuse at the two young lads, who turned straight into the onslaught that had them unconscious before they were conscious of the fight. The severity of the attack and the lack of blood in their alcohol were the two major factors that led to such a quick knock out.

I shook my head in disgust as T and D jumped and stamped on the bloodied puppets beneath them. Tony noticed my disgust as our eyes met over the roof of the car.

'When they come in tomorrow we'll give it 'em,' Tony said.

I looked again at the two bodies still being kicked around the pavement.

'We'll have to do something now Tony, they're going to kill them.'

The beating stopped at our approach. I stood in front of T and Tony D. One lad on the floor was curled up, open mouth seeping blood. The other, face squashed against the cold, wet pavement, his body starfished, pale and limp. Both were in deep sleepsville. My heart cried inside. Nobody should do this to two helpless, harmless human beings, it was wrong. T and D must have seen the disapproval we held because a look of fear overcame them.

'You're out of order,' Tony told the pair, then looked across at me, nothing spoken, but his thoughts were mine and mine his. We knew what had to be done.

'BANG!'

Tony fired a right cross that sent his man spiralling unconscious to the pavement. At exactly the same time, with exactly the same punch, I took away T's consciousness. As his body fell, a short right roundhouse kick to his face helped him on his way. My legs shook with the aftermath of adrenalin. I looked down on the four unconscious bodies that lay scattered around us, their puddled blood rippling to the raindrops. Tony looked at me and smiled,

'If the Police come now, I'm taking a dive. You can have all five of us!'

Chapter 12

Dealing with women

Prizing apart two fighting women is a tiresome and awkward task. What do you do? Where do you start? If it were two men it would be simple, you'd just manhandle them apart and physically throw them from the club/pub. How, though, can you manhandle a woman without hurting them, touching something you shouldn't touch or seeing something you shouldn't see.

Most doormen, in Coventry anyway, get a grip on a women like they would a six pack and eject tight-torn, knicker-showing bodies off the premises as physically as deemed necessary, aiming to be as non sexist as they can possibly be. Me, I find women grappling around the floor of a nightclub a problem, I probably show them too much respect, and if that's classed as being sexist then I am, and proud of it.

Tony held no such reservations. One young girl who threw racist remarks at Tony was pushed out so forcefully that when she passed me, skidding across the floormen route to the exit door, I thought she was on a skate board. Another who dared to slap Tony across the face got a slap straight back that left her, skirt around her neck, upside down on the carpet. One rather large lady bragged to Tony that she bred Rottweilers.

'Well you've got the hips for it,' he told her. He's a tall, half-caste guy of 20 stone, who looks the Afro double of Bluto of Popeye fame less the beard, skinny legs, and a huge torso, short curled black hair and the nose of a dozen boxers. One girl he was chatting to many years ago, turned out to be the 'woman' of a local heavy.

'That's my missus you're talking to,' he told Tony.

'Don't worry, you can join in and we'll gang bang her.'

When he took exception to the remark, Tony left hooked him so hard that he must have gone back in time. He was out that long that when he awoke his clothes were out of fashion.

Four steps led from the high street pavement in to the glass fronted doorway of 'Nobby's'. We, the doormen, stood at the entrance of the sticky, beer carpeted vestibule hall that led into the main bar of the pub. Being ten foot wide there was plenty of room for us to stand and check the clientele on the entrance to the establishment. I looked closely, examining Dick (an ex-doorman) and his mates, who had uninvitedly joined us for a drink.

Dick was obviously the leader as the others hung on to his every word with baited breath and obvious appreciation. He was a man I'd always got on with, but only because I'd never spent any time with him, now he just sounded aggressive and violent, slagging off all but himself. His hair and face looked just like 'action man', his arms were muscular and tattoos let only a little flesh peep out here and there. His denim bib and brace and white vest shouted out at you 'violent person'. His three friends were all hard faced affording none a smile. One in particular caught my attention. He trotted back and forward, the right side of his upper lip curled with aggression. He wanted a fight, I could see, almost smell it, he wanted to hurt someone. The menu of mayhem Dick was dishing out was making him hungry for blood. The more Dick bragged the less I thought of him, if shit could fly then this man would be squadron leader. I remember thinking that if he went on much more he'd start believing it himself. I could see my fellow doorman, Rob and Clive 'The Crook' were getting fed up with it to.

'Two women are fighting outside,' a stranger interrupted. We looked through the window.

'Do you want me to stop it Rob?' I asked. Rob brushed his blond moustache with his finger in deep thought. His blond hair, boyish looks and tall, lean physique taking ten years off his forty. He was a veteran doorman who I respected, and although he was known as a diplomat, he was also known for his fast hands when he finally did have a go.

'Have a look Geoff.' I might as well, I thought, get some fresh air. The smell of bullshit was getting too much for me. The two girls were entwined by hand and hair, knickers and torn panty hose, the whole thing looked so undignified, as usual one stiletto was missing. I heaved a heavy sigh, I hated this bit. I bent down to prize them apart, a shoe horn would have quite handy, or a bucket of cold water. Right outside the pub, as I mentioned earlier, there was a row of bus stops, people queuing, full and empty buses, all waiting and watching to see if I touched anything or saw anything I shouldn't whilst I was ungluing the pair. Just as I was about to begin the delicate separation, a gruff, aggressive and threatening voice forced its way through the knickers and knockers to arrive on the doorstep of my left ear.

'Leave them alone, let them fight.' I looked up from my semi-crouched position: it was the man with the permanently curled lip.

'Who the fuck are you?' I asked, politely. He smiled, but his lip was still curled. Perhaps it was painted on?

'Let them fight, I want to see a bit of fanny.' Nice boy. To be honest he threw me a bit. I should have just separated them, but I didn't, I paused for a moment. What's it got to do with him, I thought? At this, I parted them and after a little slanging and stiletto searching they were on their merry way. Old hair lip was still bothering me. I had my dickie bow on, he knew I was working, yet still he talked to me like a piece of shit. I watched him as he hovered around outside, staring at people, looking for a fight. He was a big lad, blond short hair, scruffy attire and an attitude, what an attitude. His fists clenched and his elbows slayed out some distance from his sides as though he was carrying buckets of water. Owen appeared on the scene from nowhere with a young lady on his arm, his hair as scruffy as ever.

'You want me to weigh him in for you Geoff?' he offered, looking down at the plaster of Paris that was protecting my broken right wrist.

'Who?' I said, pretending I didn't know.

'Him,' he replied, nodding his head towards the 'water carrier'.

'No,' I said, as I felt my fighting engine turn over in my stomach. I knew I had to deal with it myself, broken arm or not. I had done what had seemed like thousands of left hand punches since my wrist was broken, so I was pretty sure it would be alright. It probably would have been if I'd given my left a chance. As soon as 'hair lip' approached I lined him up with old faithful. My left hand might as well have been in my pocket for all the use I was giving it. His head was nodding like one of those little toy dogs you get for the back of your car, and that smile.

'Hey, sorry about that one there man.'

'Don't be sorry,' I said, tapping his belly with the back of my left hand to get my punching distance. 'Just don't tell me how to do my job again.' The familiar tunnel vision came in, all sound went out except the sound of his voice and that familiar sickly smell of violence hung in the air like a ripening pheasant corpse. He flung his arms back in a fit of exclamation, as if to say who the hell did I think I was talking to, couldn't I see how tough he was, couldn't I recognise a fighter when I saw one? No, I couldn't. The way he walked and talked, by his expressions and his attitude, by his unprepared stance and the way he was underestimating me and by the way he reeked of malice, all I could see was another fucking amateur who was about to get 'caned' couldn't he see that I'd lined him up, couldn't he see that I was getting my punching distance by tapping his stomach, couldn't he see that my humble approach was just an overcoat covering a shotgun, couldn't he see anything.

'It's not your fucking job outside,' he pointed. I tapped his stomach again, distancing is very important, I wanted to get it right. I lowered my voice slightly, mentally disarming him a little more.

'All I'm saying is, don't tell me my job, alright?' Ending my statement with a question was another ploy, as soon as you ask someone a question, be it frivolous or serious, the brain is engaged with that question, and while it is engaged for even a second, I strike. 'Bang,' a broken right-handed punch pierced the air like an arrow, hitting the target slightly high. This should have been a straight knockout, but I was a little over zealous, too keen to get it over with.

To be accurate you have to look at the target exactly where you want to hit it, looking at the jaw, then punching the jaw. I never got my targeting quite right, but it still did enough to make his brain think it was cabbage and his legs think they were jelly. He flew backwards at a rate of knots, desperately trying to regain his composure, the sardonic smile now transformed into a worried, semi conscious, bedraggled kind of look. I ran in for the kill, never one to look a gift horse in the mouth. I grasped both his shoulders to pull him into a knee attack but changed my mind at the last minute and pulled him rapidly head first into the newsagents window next to the pub. As he began his descent, I volleyed his face so hard I hurt my foot, he crashed to the ground. He was strong though and kept trying to get up, so I rained more kicks in at him. My adrenalin deafness was pierced by the sound of a woman shouting,

'Don't kick his face,' I guess it must have looked as bad as it sounds, but it could have been worse, it could have been me being kicked. I stepped back and he got back to his feet still cowering and covering his face, then scuttled off into the sunset. A friend once said to me that surely the ultimate sign of strength is the person who can take an insult and walk away, turn the other cheek in effect. In a perfect world she would be right, but on the door and with the dark side of society it doesn't work, it's not in the rules. On the door especially in Coventry City centre, your pillar of survival rests on peoples respect for you. The good majority respect you for being a gentleman, the bad minority will only give you respect if you are a fighter.

'Yea though I walk through the valley of death yet will I fear no evil, because I am the meanest bastard in the valley.'

If they see a chink in your armour then believe me that's where they will aim their poisoned darts. As I mentioned before, you are paid to protect the good majority from the bad minority. To let these people talk down to you and insult can have a devastating effect. People , good or bad, watching you turn the other cheek, will consciously or subconsciously lose respect for you and the more you turn the other cheek the more respect you lose, until all of a sudden you've lost control.

'Take no notice of him, he's a wanker, so and so backed him down last week,' and when you try to enforce your authority all you'll get is back chat, next thing you know you're out of a job because people, quite often the very people who are telling you to turn the other cheek, don't respect you enough to let you do the job. As bad as it might sound, you have to make an example of these people so that others say, 'Don't mess with him, he won't take any shit'.

To survive in a violent environment you have to be worse than the people you're dealing with. Only then can you gain respect. As for society in general, they will let you turn the other cheek, but only so that they can slap you on the other side of your face. It is admirable to take the insult, to turn and walk away, but I don't think your feet would get very far before your insulter/assailant is jumping on you from behind and battering you to a pulp. If people were nice enough to let you decline the altercation then that would be fine, but the majority won't. Why? Because these people don't see turning the other cheek as strength, they see it as a weakness. It gives them a buzz and serves as an appetiser for their ego: the main meal is showing your head the pavement.

There are still a few people out there who will let you turn and walk away, but most will not, and telling the difference between the former and the latter is an unenviable if not impossible task. So you unfortunately have to, out of necessity for survival, treat all as the former or suffer the grave consequences. But before you cast a stone at me for striking first and refusing to turn the other cheek, remember that I've been there and tried it both ways, so I think I know what works and what doesn't.

If, of course, you want to take the chance and walk, that's your prerogative, but if the problem involves your wife, daughter, husband, son mother or father etc., you've then got their safety to consider. A young local girl was attacked by three youths, beaten into a semi-conscious stupor, and had her gold front tooth pulled out with a pair of pliers. Generally speaking the people we're talking about have no morals or conscience at all and like it or not in today's society that's the shade of light we have to live under.

This actually reminds me of the pathetic specimen I read about in the national press who turned the other cheek. As a brown belt in Judo he was quoted as being an 'expert', and got battered to a pulp by three assailants. He was later quoted as saying,

'I could have hurt them badly with my Judo, but that's not the way I've been taught.' Had he been honest he would have said something along the lines of,

'I would have liked to have defended myself with my basic knowledge of Judo, but basically I was scared shitless and didn't have the bottle.' Perhaps he didn't have the bottle to be honest either.

A good example of respect, I guess, was the incident I had with the two policewomen at an acid party. Actually, whilst on the subject of acid parties, I might as well give you might opinion of them, because they do get a very bad press. Drugs are definitely taken there and by the lorry load. In fact, the people taking them are probably in the majority rather than the minority, and an acid do without them would be like a kid's birthday party without the sweets and cake.

You can tell most people are on them because they are 'out there with Pluto', but the dealers are very discreet and professional, never forcing their wares (though in these places they don't need to). I personally am against drugs and think the dealers peddle in misery, but that's their right in a free society to do and take whatever they desire, so who am I to blow against the wind?

I think putting drugs into your body is like putting diesel into a petrol engine. It's ironic that these people will go out on a Sunday afternoon and meticulously clean and polish their cars inside and out, yet treat their own bodies like nuclear tips. If parts on the car start to wear or break they'll replace them or even change their car for a newer model. You can't do this with your own body when bits start to go. You only get one issue, and if people want to fuck themselves up then who am I to lecture them to put it right? A punch on the nose is all I'd get for my trouble.

Violence, though, from my experience, doesn't happen often at these parties. The drugs seem to suppress the aggression, and from the way they all dance it's not surprising they don't have any energy left for fighting. The Eclipse night club is a different kettle of fish. The owners there, who are personal friends of mine, frown upon the use of drugs on their premises, handing over any dealers caught to the police or giving them a bit of backroom treatment. This is the way forward, nip it in the bud. Cut the dealers out of the body of society like the cancer that they are. Surveys show that most violent attacks, robbery, rapes etc., are performed whilst under the influence of an illegal substance.

It's not only the punters, though. Some doormen, maybe even the majority of them, smoke dope or take speed or often steroids to give them the courage without which they wouldn't 'bounce', courage that they wouldn't have without the drug. They are cowardly lions, cowering on the yellow brick road of life, but the land of Oz here isn't a diamond sparkling emerald city in which life thrives, it is some dark, putrid tin can alley where life dies and the wizard isn't a kindly, old, balding man giving you a witch-destroying task, he is a gold-braceleted, flash-dressing, smooth-talking rep from the dark side of life. His only interest is your money and the task he gives is one of soul-destroying and the courage that's gained in only on loan until the morning, replaced by a low that is lower than the high is high. Every incident I've ever dealt with and every fight I've ever fought was done when I was straight. I've never needed any help from the evil weed.

As a culmination to 'dealing with women', I must tell you about 'Radio Rental Rob' who as I mentioned before could motor with the best of them but was more of a lover than a fighter and he did like to 'deal' with women. I've got to say that Rob was the funniest, strangest man that I've ever come across: he always joked around. He was, nay, is, old for a doorman at 40, though, as I mentioned before, he does look a lot younger. If you checked out his attire however, you might guess his age. In all the years that I have known him he has always worn exactly the same clothes. He has never changed but he has always looked dead smart in an old-fashioned sort of way with his black patent leather shoes, dark, policeman-type trousers and a white collarless shirt that proudly held his black dickie-bow.

Sometimes, if he didn't like the music being played by the band or the DJ he would think nothing of sticking some great big pieces of toilet roll in his ears to show his disapproval. This always got a laugh from us. The management wasn't so happy about it though - Rob was on the floor more time than the cleaner's hoover. His party trick was to put raw sausages into a punter's coat pocket while it hung in the G's cloak room, then watch in amusement as they jumped out of their skins on discovering raw meat wrapped around their comb or hairslide. Sometimes, in wonder, we'd follow the punters outside, waiting for them to put their cold hands into their warm pockets then screeching with laughter when they screamed at the feel of the flesh-like sausage. I know that it may sound disgusting but Rob would think nothing of putting a half-eaten pie or pizza in a punter's pocket, then laugh himself silly all night just thinking about the reaction it would provoke upon its discovery.

He also has an uncanny knack of seeing celebrity likenesses in may of the punters who came and left but you'd never see it until Rob pointed it out. One old, little, scruffy lady who smelled like piss and used Nobby's for a while was, I lie not, a carbon copy of 'Wordsworth', the elderly woman prisoner of the Australian soap: Prisoner Cell Block H. Every time that she walked through the entrance way of Nobby's, Rob's eyes would light up and yell at her,

'Get back to your cell, Wordsworth.' Even she used to laugh at him. We'd be in mid-conversation and Rob would suddenly yell and point, 'Alan Whicker' and, low and behold, Alan's double would be walking past the door and we'd all erupt in fits of laughter. His coup-de-grace however, came in the pokey 6'6" cloakroom in G's nightclub. His lady at the time was a sweet-looking, tiny, pretty little button of a girl dressed all in black in the style of eighties punk rockers. Her body was tight and cute but her mouth was absolutely foul: she'd say things that would shock me. She worked there as a cloakroom attendant and, on giving one young man back his coat at the end of the night he asked cheerfully,

'What put that smile on your face?' The same face transformed from sweet to evil and replied,

'Spunk.'

The night was drawing to a close so the lady in black, Radio Rental, the receptionist from the hole in the wall opposite the cloakroom and myself awaited the 2 a.m. rush for coats. Rob was pushing his lady around inside the cloakroom in a jovial way.

'If you keep fucking me about I'll take your dick out and suck you off in front of everyone,' she shouted. Nice girl, I thought.

'Go on then,' dared Rob, hands on hips, pushing his midriff towards her.

'Yeah, go on,' I added, knowing that she wouldn't have the nerve. What did I know? I watched in disbelief as she slowly knelt before him and, with a deeply seductive look, she tantalisingly unzipped the prison that held his ever growing one eyed monster that must have thought that it was his birthday. As she took him in her mouth, letting the entire length slide past her lips, then retracting and licking it all around as her left hand pulled him backwards and forwards. Their closed eyes opened quickly as Carol, the stunned shocked receptionist, screamed in horror and ran from her little room opposite. The management, of course, didn't take kindly to Rob's antics and sacked him on the spot. Didn't he know that oral sex wasn't allowed at work?

Chapter 13

The hunters and the hunted

In Coventry there are a number of quality doormen who work all over the city, but when a 'team' is required and the phone rings, they all become as one. The girl friends and wives get let down and all the 'doors' are abandoned until the dirty deed is done. In the late 80's especially, it would be nothing to see 50 top doormen on the rampage looking to right a wrong. The police knew about us and were not very happy about our presence, but could do little or nothing to stop us. We were a law unto ourselves. If someone needed sorting or a pub needed protection from threatening gangs, we would get together and sort it. We were strong, too strong really. More often than not our presence alone was enough and strong arm tactics did not need to be employed.

If a team was needed, Big Al did the organising. He was probably the most respected doorman in the city whose 'rep' extended to far greater boundaries. I had the pleasure of working with him for many years at the Pippin. He was a mountain of a man, whose skin lay blacker than ash and standing six feet four and weighing in at 22 stone, he was far from slight. He was charismatic in the greatest degree and cooler than iced water and although a powerful fighter, that was not where his greatest strength lay. A maker of great friends and a diplomat, his real power lay in the fact that he made a bad, bad enemy who conceded to no one and nothing. The word in Coventry was 'don't fuck with this man'.

The ring of the phone broke the warm, centrally heated silence in the front room of my terraced, suburban three bedroomed abode. My body refused to rise from its wonderfully comfortable semi reclined position on the couch and my wife reluctantly left her seat to answer it. And why not? She couldn't possibly be as comfortable as me. No sooner had she put the phone to her ear, she pushed it away again and her face grimaced.

'It's Al for you.'

She didn't need to tell me because I knew by her look and manner. My Ex was small and Orientally pretty, but held a giant slaying appetite for martial dominance with the back up of an acidic temper. Not the beautiful, gentle creature I fell in love with 10 years before, but then again, I wasn't the sweet, soft 18 year old boy that she had married.

As soon as she said it was Al I knew and she knew what the phone call meant. We were to meet tomorrow at the Holy Head pub. I've had many such phone calls over the years and although they always caused arguments in my abode, I still went. It was expected of you, the price you pay, I'm afraid, for 'belonging.' You could decline of course and make your excuses, but if you did it was remembered and after a couple of such refusals you would no longer 'belong.'

'One day I might need a team myself,' I argued. 'If I don't go when they ask me they won't come out for me when I need them.'

My Ex hated the 'teams' going out, hated the door, but more than anything she hated the back bone the door was giving me. Before working the door I was very reluctant to argue with her when we fell out and backed down at every 'meet'. I had become frightened of the very girl I once adored. Although she probably didn't realise it she was, because of my wimpiness, subconsciously losing all respect for me. Fortunately for me, unfortunately for her, the ever growing confidence that door work was feeding me spilled over into my home life. The worm turned and so began the decline of my marriage.

John was a rugged, pit faced, mean looking kind of guy on the surface, but underneath, a nice chap. He headed the door at the Holly Head and it was for him that we were congregating. He'd run in with a group of local heavies who frequented the place and in the middle of an altercation John broke the nose of their leader, who understandably was none too happy. The issue ended with some heavy threats of guns and the like. Threats after such incidents are always cast, but very rarely followed up - talk is very cheap. However, this time they were followed up and followed up again by more and more threats, which absolutely, indubitably would be backed by violence on Saturday night, at least that's what everyone said. The gang in question had a heavy reputation in the area and were well known for follow ups and home visits, so the 'A' team were needed.

I arrived at the Holly Head, a huge detached premises set back off a cross-roaded dual carriage way, just outside the city centre. Porsche and BMW were the norm in the spacious car park of this oh so posy, trendy, popular pub, where vests and summer shorts were worn all year round. Every man looked as though he'd just got a four week tan in the Bahamas and every woman like she'd just spent half a day in the beauty parlour - Vogue on the outside, vague on the inside. Physically they were the creme de la creme of this three spired, Cov capped, once thriving, now diving industrious city. But to me they didn't seem like real people. They were plasticky, posh and unapproachable. I'm working class and proud of the fact. I don't like snobs, but that's enough of the chip on my shoulder.

A dozen of us walked through the high arched entrance way to be welcomed by a black suited, dicky bowed doorman. A circular bar sat in the middle of the room that was filled with oldy, worldy memorabilia. An old fashioned, red telephone box sat proudly in the corner; animal busts lurched out of wall at you wherever you looked and the carpet was deep piled and smooth, not beer stick like most pubs. The people of plastic seemed in the minority tonight, swamped by the dozens and dozens of doormen on call. All the drinks were on the house courtesy of the management.

I looked around. Every face was familiar. I didn't envy anyone who got on the wrong side of this crowd. Patiently we all waited for a foe we all knew would not arrive, if they had any sense. Anyway, we were in all modesty, the elite and they and everybody else in the city knew it, but we had to be there just in case. The sound of breaking glass, usually the doorman's first warning of a fight, killed the conversation deader than a newspapered fly. In seconds 20 doormen surrounded two bewildered, quarrelling women in the greatest display of overkill that I have ever had the pleasure of witnessing. That was to be the highlight of the night because our sparring partners didn't arrive for what would have been a grave mistake anyway. Some people won't be warned off though. Some people have to be hurt.

Matey was tall and lean with professional hands that put themselves on anybody that dared to cross him, and if the people crossing him became too small in number, he would put them on innocent by-standers as a top-up for his ego, practice and reputation. He was obese in his talent for hurting people. He thrived on fear. The feeling he got when he walked into a pub or club splattered his whole inside with a pleasure that can only be likened to an orgasm. When you've got a person who enjoys violence and knows how to dish it out you have a psychopath and a very dangerous person.

He always stood in suede hiking boots that had the wearing of ten Brecon Beacon walks. His trousers, baggy and unironed, were not as wrinkled as his face which was like a bulldog chewing a wasp. His hair was ink black and cropped. Everyone has the right to be ugly, but this man abused the privilege. He had a bounce in his walk which was arrogance exemplified. He was one of a gang of four that always hung around together and made enemies like tycoons make profit.

G made a very bad enemy and Matey unwittingly signed his own death warrant and penned the beginnings of his own obituary when his Brecon boots strode him through the swing doors and across the Axminster carpet of G's nameless establishment. G and T were the best gaffers I'd worked for: nice people, two of the very few people who knew the worth of a good doorman. G was not a 'fighter', though he could fight, and if you made an enemy of him it was your fault. I'd never seen him cross anyone that wasn't completely out of order. He stood five feet, eight inches, and was naturally stout with a Toby jug face. As with most naturally stout people he was and is always 'gonna start a diet' and 'gonna start training'.

What he lacked in physique, though, he doubles in heart and character and is a veritable dictionary of stories and jokes. He swears that when his mate took the clock out of his BMW in order to wind back the mileage before its sale, there was a sticker on the back saying 'Oh no, not again'. Amicable he was, but gullible he definitely wasn't. So when our friend started trying to 'paint the pen' the colour he wanted, G told him in no uncertain terms that it jolly well wasn't on, or words to that effect. No one else before this point had enough moral fibre to tell him 'how it was', but G scored it as he saw it.

Matey's face smiled an evil smile. 'More sport,' he thought to himself. That familiar rush of blood he liked so much made a welcome return, and his fast right shot from his hip with ferocious velocity. G, who had half-expected it, charged inside, wrestling him to the floor with a shoulder barge. Within milliseconds the two doorman who had been close by were all over him like a rash, frenziedly punching and kicking their prey to unconsciousness, then flailing his limp body down the three steps outside onto the cobbled pavement, whiplashing his head into the stones, the hollow echo of his skull pathetic and sickly.

They watched his lifeless body for a moment. Nothing. They felt the ever so familiar tingle of adrenalin-induced relief in their stomachs, then fear at the realisation of what they had done, who they had done.

'Fuck him,' G said, as he ushered the doormen back inside. 'Let the bastard die.'

G was always a thoughtful soul. This may all sound very callous, and of course it is, but you simply cannot treat lowlife of this calibre with kid gloves.

The whole town lived and lay in fear of him. Every weekend and often in the week too he would savagely damage somebody. He never queued for anything, and would 'level' anyone who challenged his right. The previous week he broke a man's nose in three places - the bar, the lounge and the car park - for holding his gaze too long. Everyone up until now who opposed him was punished.

The curtained glass front door at the pub entrance screamed discontent as its belly exploded, spitting a million fragments of glass in every direction as reimbursement in the guise of a home-made petrol bomb crashed through. The curtain engulfed into a flaming sunset and the fire slid across the petrol-soaked carpet like a gauntlet in hell. G ran bare-foot down the stairs, wielding the baseball bat that stood guard by his bed, his heart trying, it seemed, to beat its way out of his chest. Bats may be good for hitting people with, but they're not very good for putting out fires, so he quickly exchanged it for a red, foam fire extinguishers that hung nearby on the wall.

The fire was crackling and eating away at the wood door and the delicious carpet. The foam shot from the nozzle of the extinguisher and attacked the flames quickly and effectively, quelling the spread and blanketing all. The fire was out. G's heart was nearly out as well, out of his chest. T approached from behind him, feeding her arm around his pyjama'd body, massaging his chest sympathetically. They stared at the charred remains of their entrance way, realising that it could have been them, their children, their lives. Both knew who and why. He breathed a deeper sigh than he could ever remember breathing. This was war.

Saturday evening, early, six o' clock. The one hundred year old stone-blocked public house sat empty in the solitude of contentment, the calm before the storm. The teak wooden bar that carried every optic conceivable to man was almost ghostly in its emptiness. The carpet was busy pushing out the aroma of last night's spilled beer and smoke.

G sat at a silent table of four. T and the two kids had learned from experience when and when not to speak. He forked his dinner from middle to edge and edge to middle of his plate. T knew when she cooked it that he wouldn't eat it but still she cooked it. He knew when she put it on the table that he wouldn't eat it but still he took it and thanked her for it. It was a facade, a game you play when worry slays the appetite. Just go on as normal and pretend it's alright and it will be, maybe. Two pretty daughters seemed impervious to it all, tucking into their meals, but subconsciously it was there, moulding their little minds, taking notes, making observations. The experiences will come in handy when they're older. Is it right, though, to infest their little minds with such horrors, or are we mollycoddling them into unpreparedness if we protect them from life?

G's dinner lay scrapped in the bottom of the dustbin as a reminder that this situation, which had brewed and matured in this area since Matey pushed through puberty, had to be resolved, and not verbally. His mind was confused. What to do, what to do? He searched the annals of his mind for the answer. He'd trod this path many times before today and knew the answer before the search, but just didn't want to hear it. Last time he swore to himself it would be the last time. That's the carrot you dangle to your mind when it's turmoiled with trouble, 'Just hold on and this will be the last time, after this we'll pull away from it all. Just do it this last time.' But even when you're telling yourself it's the last time you know it's not. It can never be.

Seven o' clock, almost time to open. God, it had been a long wait. Time distortion had been pushing swords in and out of his heart all day. He just wanted it to be over. The heavy rapping of the front door sent his adrenalin into overdrive. He knew before he unbolted and creaked open the new heavy oak door who it would be, but he was glad to get it over and done with. If this bastard wanted to fight he'd absolutely come to the right place. Matey stood menacingly at the top of the steps, the run of his 'I'm back' smile broken only by the golf ball thick lip that rose to almost touch the hanging swell of his storm blue, bloodshot right eye.

Three companions lined the bottom step ready to war. Bat, bar, and knife were openly displayed in a blatant show of arrogance for G, the law, and life in general. G tried to hide the quickening of his breathing with a sigh that seemed to say 'Tut, tut, I thought you'd learned your lesson. He steadied it, controlled it, then raised his finger, pointing, hoping that the shake he felt through his whole body wouldn't show. His eyes widened in mock surprise.

'There's something different about you today. How are you anyway? Last time I saw you you were unconscious.'

As the angry steam was about to blow from Matey's ear, Dave, a short, very stocky Judo man and Pete, a taller, athletic-looking type, emerged from the pub either side of G.

'You met the lads, haven't you?'

The words were still in the air as Matey's fist sent G down but not out. He grabbed Matey's legs rugby style and the pair crashed down the steps. Dave missiled a heavy glass beer jug from the top of the steps with as much force as he could muster, crashing into the head of the knife wielder just as his arm was rising in a stabbing motion toward G, who was rolling and thrashing around the cobbled stone with Matey. In an involuntary action the knife fell from his hand as his fingers stretched in shock. He screamed in a high-pitched banshee voice then screamed again and again and again, then danced, hands holding head, trying to stop the pain and secretion of blood through the skull and hair, round and round like a child in a tantrum.

Pete fenced with his fellow batsman, wood thunking wood. Dave cleared all three steps to grab no.3, taking him over with an ogoshi hip throw, diverting his head into the cobbles as he fell.

'Police!' came a cry from nowhere. Everyone scattered except old 'head wound', who was still performing a screaming tribal war dance.

'I'll be back with a shooter, you bastard,' G heard as the door closed behind him. The blood on the cobbled stone was still scarletly warm as the lads necked their third pint, a celebration drink. G also ate while his appetite still allowed him. Round two to G.

The morning started at an early five o' clock. Sleepless nights were another by-product of worry and stress, but he didn't complain - he'd been there before. He and worry were friends, sleeping partners. He could handle it. Anyway, it was character building.

Funny thing was, though, all these tests and tasks that purported to build your mind seemed at the same time to destroy your body. Many pub landlords die of heart attacks or develop ulcers or suffer nervous breakdowns, but the breweries are very sympathetic. As long as these ailments don't occur during working hours they don't mind. There was no use lying in bed thinking about it all. If you leave your mind to itself it will dwell on misery and spiral you down into ever increasing unhappiness.

So he climbed out of bed, pulled back a curtain slightly and wiped a peephole in the condensation on the window. Even from up here he could see the thick, congealed blood on the ground below, a reminder of last night and a reminder that it wasn't over. He could get the police involved, but that wouldn't help any more than telling a school teacher when your child is being bullied. It just shows your antagonist that you're scared and can't handle the situation.

Reports all day and for the rest of the week came into the pub that Matey was up to something and it was heavy. Not just idle chat: he had it from very good sources that Matey was in pursuit of a gun. G came to the conclusion that this man was not going to be stopped in the usual manner. If he wants to play with guns, let's play with guns. It's like a game of crap. If you want to win and take the prize you have to 'see' your opponent every time, whether you have a good hand or a bad, see him all the way through no matter what the stakes, and just hope that if you can't call his bluff your hand is better than his.

If there's one thing you do pick up in the pub trade, it's contacts. One phonecall to an old friend in Touster, Northamptonshire, and a gun was acquired. £150 bought him a Sauer & Sauer semi-automatic hand gun. The credits were over, the main film was about to begin. T wasn't happy about the introduction of 'lead', but G assured her it was the only way, and anyway he was only going to scare him with it. But it would be loaded, just in case.

Surprisingly, our friend lived in a nice residential part of the town, the address acquired through another contact at the Post Office. G, Dave and Pete sat in a 'borrowed' car down a little industrial estate side road, just outside Matey's estate. He was known to walk this way on a Friday, on his way into town. The moon was full and the air had a November coldness that chattered G's teeth. Dave and Pete sat in the back seat. Dave sported a sheepskin with the collar turned up high, hiding his face and almost meeting the rim of his black, knitted pom-pom hat. Pete's donkey jacket collar was equally high, his black leather gloves shielding his fingers from the cold. G's coloured shell-suit top was hardly a match for the warmth and disguise of his partners in crime.

He touched the cold steel of the killing machine lying dormant in his pocket. This would be the last round. He thought back to the warmth of his bed, Tracy, the kids. His bubble burst as Matey bounced around the corner directly behind them. 'I wish that fucking moonlight would disappear - we're almost spotlighted here.' Matey's mind must have been a million miles away not to see them in this otherwise barren side road. G watched him in the rear view mirror, all readied themselves.

As soon as he was alongside the car the flew out at him, punching and pulling him to the ground. Dave grabbed his kicking legs, Pete the back collar of his leather coat, pulling him along the tarmac to somewhere secluded, his face and knuckles ripping and grazing along the way. His frenzied struggling met a hefty kick from the steel toe-capped boots G wore especially for the occasion. He struggled less, but breathed in short, sharp bursts.

This was a field he'd never played in before. It was a big field and he was a small, lost child. He didn't like it one bit. They dragged him down a small gravelled alley between two newly-built factory units that barely had room for them all. Pete, held his body to the floor by pinning the neck of his jacket to the ground, while Dave sat on his legs. G hovered over him masterfully, smiling. He knew now by the pathetic look on Matey's face that this was the final blow in what seemed like a long, long round.

G slowly pulled out the gun and showed it to the quivering wreck that lay before him. His eyes shot forward to the front of their sockets in disbelief. His mouth motioned words that wouldn't, couldn't come out. Only dribble ran down the side of his mouth, like a rat leaving a sinking ship. G didn't feel frightened anymore, he felt an almost uncontrollable, indescribable surge of power rush through his body, and dark, sinister voice in the back of his head saying, 'Shoot him, shoot him, shoot him'.

'This time it's for keeps,' he said. 'You've upset too many people so you're gonna have to go.' He thrust the barrel of the gun into Matey's mouth, busting his lip and breaking his teeth en route, and held it there for some agonising seconds. Matey's life rushed before him and steam rose from his trousers where his bladder had emptied itself.

'Fucking kill him,' urged Dave. 'Go on, kill him. Give me the gun, I'll do it.'

Matey's eyes stretched to the farthest corners of their sockets to try to see Dave's face to see if he was bluffing or for real. If he was bluffing it was a good bluff. His muffled cries, like those of a trapped puppy, brought G, who by now was really considering killing him, to his senses. Retracting the bloodied nozzle of the gun from his mouth he concluded,

'Naa, he's not worth it. I think he's learnt a lesson. You come within a mile of my gaff again and next time it'll be for keeps.'

Matey's body shook with relief as he wept. G never saw or heard from him again.

That, of course, was an extremity. It's not often that you have to go that far. Every case is judged on its merits, like for example, the time I had a cheque stolen from the bedsit I was living in.

I was 'on the sick' from my labouring job at a factory after a second operation on my broken arm. As a result of my incapacity to work, the council were kindly sending me a cheque for £120 a month to cover the said bedsit. The phrase 'not enough room to swing a cat' must almost definitely have been coined in this 12 foot by 12 foot room that boasted nothing more than that. The mid-terraced, grubby, pre-war house was on the very edge of town in bedsit land, in a street that was never less than double parked from one end to the other. The dilapidated, crumbling front garden wall did little to hide the torn dustbin bags and the litter-strewn, tiny grassless garden that really did need hiding. The back gaden was worse, and was the home for an army of rats that terrorized the cats. The previous occupant of my room was a non paying, young female prostitute, so as you can imagine, the bed had a strong and interesting history, plus of course, a spring-worn mattress.

The carpet was at least a hundred years old and had more holes in it than a string vest. The electric meter only ever ran out in the middle of a great film when you had no 50 pence pieces left. There was an electric wire that seemed to go from nowhere to nowhere and was held together by sellotape and ran under the carpet by the sink, peeping through at every hole. It seemed to be keeping guard by the sink, zapping and throwing you across the room if you dared to put a bare foot on it after a shower or wash. I learnt from experience that it was best to stand on the bed to dry yourself after a shower and not use the sink unless you were wearing rubber boots. But it was home.

The problem with the communal door was the communal letterbox. Sometimes the mail would disappear before it hit the chipped stone tiles under the letter box, although up until now, mine had not been touched. A week after my cheque was due I rang the council to complain and they informed me that not only had the cheque been sent, but that it had been cashed as well. Everybody in the bedsit knew me, so I was more than a little offended when they confirmed what I had already suspected - it had been stolen.

One by one I confronted everyone in the house and they all vigorously denied any knowledge of the cheque, but I still told them what I was going to do to the guilty person when I found them and I was going to find them. My main suspect was the gangling youth in the room next to me. He was six feet two and built like a vertical clothes line. He was a known cheque thief, but he knew me from the town and repeatedly denied the theft. He was pretty convincing, but remained on my short list of suspects.

On visiting the council, who would not give me a replacement cheque over the counter thank you very much, I was given a photocopy of the said cheque, cashed in the name of T.J. Goss into an account at Lloyds Bank. The next hour saw me and Sharon at the counter of Lloyds insisting to talk to the manager or failing that, somebody else in authority. There was no one there - the manager was in a meeting (aren't they always?). The young man I spoke to would confirm that the cheque had been cashed in the said account, but he could not, due to regulations, give me that person's address. I knew the lad's face from when I worked in G's, so I chanced my arm. I leant over my face closer to the glass partition and whispered,

'Look, you know me. Just write his name on a piece of paper so I can sort it out, no one will know.'

He looked around him and thought for a minute, then began scribbling on a scrap of paper. He pushed it under the glass partition.

'Be careful, it's my job,' he said.

The house was in Longford, my neck of the woods. I knew the area well, though the name I was holding didn't ring a bell. With Sharon at my side, I knocked on the door of this modest, terraced house, my heart pounding that familiar pound. No answer. I knocked again. Still no answer. The house was on the end of the terrace with a back entry, mud road between this and the next row of houses on this busy main road. I skipped over a little garden wall to my left and walked up the side road to the back of the house to check it out. No one there, just a line of blowing washing and a child's slide. We made our way back to the car.

'I'll come back later,' I told Sharon.

She'd only come along for the experience. One live situation was worth a hundred manufactured gym fights.

Two hours later, keen to conclude this unhappy saga, I knocked on the door again, heart beating at a rate of knots. My face, hard with anger as the door opened, put a worried look on the face of the lovely lady who answered it. My soft voice soothed her a little.

'Is Mr Goss home?' I asked.

'Oh yes,' she replied. 'Fred, someone's at the door for you,' she shouted up the stairs directly behind her. 'Come in a minute.'

I thanked her and stood in the small, carpeted, neat hallway. I made a mental note of the baseball bat standing guard by the stairs. Fred came down, shirtless, his dark skin and shoulder length hair put me in mind of an apache Indian. His voice sounded shaky. He tried to hide it,

'Come in,' he said, as he walked into the front room and sat down in an armchair of dark brown chord.

'What can I do for you?'

I unfolded the photo copy of my beloved cheque and handed it to him.

'I've come to sort this out,' I answered.

He looked at it. He knew what it was and I knew he knew, but he wasn't about to admit it so he had to play the game. He refolded the paper and handed it back to me.

'I run a second hand shop, so I see a lot of cheques. I don't remember this one,' he said, shrugging his shoulders unconvincingly.

'My name is Geoff Thompson and that's a photocopy of my cheque. It was stolen from me. I want it back and I want the person who stole it from me,' I said, very matter-of-factly and with no hint of kindness in my voice.

'I'll tell you what. Come to my shop tomorrow and I'll go through my invoice book with you so we can see who brought it in. I've got a feeling this one brought a video with it, but I can't be sure until I look in my book. Come in tomorrow.'

Realising that he hadn't had my cheque personally and that he was just a middle man, I apologised for the intrusion of his privacy. I knew the score. I knew that second hand dealers dealt with stolen Giro cheques, selling goods for them or even buying them for a fraction of their worth, but this didn't concern me. As I said, he was just the middle man. I wanted the man that sold it to him.

The large second hand shop stood oddly next to a fish and chip shop and in the middle of a very rough area in the south of the city.

Lawn mowers, garden equipment and cabinets sat outside like orphans looking for new homes. Inside was everything from fourth hand weights to second hand wedding rings. Fred busied himself round the shop, trying to be cool, as though not bothered by my presence. I knew he was and they'll have told him,

'Give him what he wants, he's bad news.'

'What have you got for me Fred,' I asked.

He wouldn't look me in the eye.

'Well, I've had a look in my books and I was right, he did buy a video with it, but I can't remember the lad very well. He hasn't been in here much, I'm sorry I can't help you more.'

He was playing my game, but wasn't in my league.

'Look Fred, I know you know who he is and I respect you for not wanting to grass him up and I don't want to fall out with you because you're just the middle man, but I'm gonna keep coming in here 'til you tell me and I know you won't want that 'cus it's bad for business. I don't care who he is or who he knows. I'm gonna find him and destroy him.'

He looked at the floor.

'I don't need the grief myself man, I've just come out from an 18. I need peace.'

I never replied.

'Look, come back tomorrow. I'll see what I can do.'

I knew he was on the run. He was scared of me, but he didn't want to get the name of a grass as that's the worst name you can get in a business of this nature. He was still worried when he went home. He didn't need this shit.

'John, who the fuck's this Geoff Thompson geezer?' he asked his brother-in-law over the phone. 'He's giving me grief at the shop over a stolen cheque of his that I bought off some guy.'

'What does he want Fred?' John asked.

Fred replied,

'He wants to know who I bought it off, but I didn't want to grass the lad up.'

John warned,

'If you don't want to get filled in Fred, I'd tell the man. He's really heavy in this town, with some heavy connections. I know him well, don't fuck with him. Tell him or he'll hurt you.'

'No, I can't grass the lad up, it's not me.'

I admired him for his bottle, he wasn't going to scare easily. I must admit, I didn't like the fact he touched my cheque, but I did like him. He was a real character and had balls, but business is business. I made my mind up to give him an ultimatum. Give me the name, or it's you. I inked my own name and address onto a stamped white envelope and inside I placed a piece of white blank paper. My plan was to give this to Fred and tell him to mail it to me within one week, putting the name I wanted on the paper. If I didn't receive it within one week, I was going to come back and wreck the shop and take my money from him. I took a deep breath as I entered the shop. As soon as Fred saw me he made a B-line for me. I didn't have to speak or threaten and I was glad I liked him.

'I've asked everyone around the town about you, your name is Good. They all said you should know.'

I suppressed my delight,

'So who is it?'

'Paul,' he said.

As I drove back to bed sit land I mulled it over again and again in my mind. I couldn't believe this skinny bastard had crossed me. I just couldn't believe the gall of the man. He was, I surmised, lower than an ants testicles. I was disappointed in him and he was going to have to be taught a lesson. My knock on the bed sit door received no reply, so I kicked the door down, surprisingly easy.

His room was smaller than mine, but an Aladdin's cave of expensive electrical gear, some boxed, stereo, telly and video in use. If he wasn't in tonight when I came back, I'll empty the place as reimbursement for my loss, I decided. The only thing that stopped me doing it now was the fact that his young, blonde girlfriend, who was so sweet, lived with him. He'd swore on his mother's life that he would never steal again if she'd only stay with him. Love isn't blind, it's downright stupid and anyway, I didn't want to hurt her.

Night in this hovel house was pretty dismal, bringing depression quicker than rigor mortis in death. I'd lay in bed, begging for sleep to take me away from it, seeking escapism in my dreams, only to find depression hovering over me when I awoke in the morning. I knocked on his mended, but still splintered door. He opened it just enough to poke his head out. He saw anger written on my face, but maintained his cool.

'Geoff, you alright?'

I answered his question with a question.

'I think you've got something to tell me, haven't you Paul?'

He came into the hallway and closed the door behind him, hiding his deceit from blondie. He looked frightened and so he should be. I was going to batter him. I poked his chest.

'You've had my cheque!'

He thrust his fingertips to his chest as though to say 'who me?'

'No man, not me, I wouldn't do that to you Geoff.'

I had planned to knock him out on the landing, but he must have guessed he was going to have some because he kept moving around me as I lined him up. He'd obviously been beaten up before.

'Come down stairs man. Let's talk outside. I don't want her to hear,' he nodded to his room.

I knew he didn't want her to hear, but that wasn't why he wanted to go outside. He wanted to go outside because he thought he'd be safe out there, that I wouldn't hit him in public, would I? His second ploy was to sit on the garden wall. Surely I wouldn't hit him whilst he was sitting down. His third ploy was to take off his glasses and wipe the lenses, not because they needed cleaning, but because he wanted to underline the fact he was wearing glasses. Nobody would hit a man with glasses on. He'd definitely been beaten up before! I pointed again,

'You had my money. I want it back.'

His voice was sympathetically high,

'No Geoff, I never. I didn't do it. Listen, I've got a deal going down that owes me a lot of coin. I'll give you some of that if you're tight.'

I shook my head in disgust.

'So you never had my cheque, but you're prepared to give me some money anyway, out of the goodness of your heart?'

He knew the game was up, but he gave it one last shot.

'I never had it Geoff. On my mother's life.'

His voice quivered. This may have worked with her indoors, but not with me. I knew he was going to have to be hit, but his cowering was putting me off. I didn't want to hit him, God I must be getting soft in my old age, but the trouble was, if I didn't hit him, he would have got away with it and he needed teaching a lesson. But I just couldn't wind myself up for it. I was beginning to feel sorry for him.

'How much money have you got?'

He must have seen the sympathy in my eyes.

'None man, not a penny.'

BANG!

A left hook dived into the side of his head, shooting his glasses off and across the other side of the road. His body rocked back, then forward.

'Get up that fucking flat now and get my money!' I screamed in anger, underlining it with a left roundhouse kick that buried itself into his belly.

For a second I saw anger in his eye. I thought he might have a go back, but that would have been just the excuse I needed to really hurt him, then break off his stealing fingers and I would have done. Sometimes I hated the dark side of myself that had been developed through necessity, by the very type that winged before me. One day, I promised myself, I will pull away from this badness and put the evil in me to sleep forever, but I knew Coventry would never let me do that. I guess he saw this though, because he retreated quicker than the Italian army, putting his hand into his back pocket and withdrawing a wad of notes. He shook as he handed it across to me, his eyes begging me not to take it off him. I counted it. Only a ton.

'There's not enough here, there's twenty short.'

His hand exclaimed 'that's all I've got man. I've got nothing left.' I stuck it in my pocket and his eyes followed my hand to my pocket, then rose to my face.

'Geoff, I haven't got any food in the house. I haven't even got a pint of milk in the fridge.'

I was hard. I had to be.

'So what. You should have thought about that when you stole my money. I owe you nothing, nothing.'

His eyes dropped to the floor and I thought of his lady upstairs, with no food or drink, suffering for his mistakes. The good in me over-ruled the bad. I took the money back out of my pocket, counted thirty notes and shoved it back at him.

'You be at the Red Lion tomorrow night with fifty or I'll hunt you down and hurt you. Next time I'll do the job properly. I must be getting soft in my old age,' I said as I walked away.

He did, of course, bring the balance the next night.

'You won't tell anyone about this, will you Geoff?' he asked.

'No,' I said.

But it was too late. I'd already told the world - his name was dirt.

Epilogue

I searched high and low and far and wide for many years to find the literary answers to the questions, worries, fears and misconceptions that I held concerning combat and its workings. I read many books on fighting and fighters, some of which purported to hold the answers to the questions that I posed. How do I overcome / control fear? How will I actually feel when confronted by a violent or potentially violent altercation? Which of my many long serving techniques would be of use to me in any given live situation? How will I know when a situation requires a physical response? And so on. Most of the books I read were interesting, even informative, but none, not a single one told me what I wanted to know. My hunger for the elusive information grew so strong that I decided to seek the answers out for myself. Many of the authors I read from and of knew nothing of the answers to my questions, others I suspected did, but for reasons that escape me, not include them in their manuscript. When I find the answers, I told myself, I'll write a book and unreservedly and unashamedly put it in print so that the many thousands of Karateka, Judo and Aikido players, boxers, wrestlers and indeed the general public can read and learn from it.

Working as a doorman in Coventry City centre answered all of my questions, sometimes brutally to the full. I learned, at times through severe hardship, that anyone can be and learn anything they wish. If you can stand the heat of the forge you can mould yourself into what ever person you so desire. A soft person can become hard, a weak person strong. This is the book that eluded my long search.

My brutal honesty and occasional overzealousness may, I know, have sounded a little blaspheming at times. If so, and if offence has been taken, I sincerely apologise. My aim was only to educate people in the workings of violence so that when the said cancer grows, as it unfortunately will into the limbs and joints of the few in society who have been spared and may not have met its

mighty wrath, they will at least be able to recognise the symptoms
and treat it early with a heavy dose of counter violence or whatever
other remedy they deem appropriate.

I have stated throughout the book that I am anti violence in that
I believe violence should only be used as a last resort. Why then,
you may well ask, do I use the medium of violence so readily? The
simple answer to that question is survival. I believe that if you
cannot resolve an altercation verbally and in your heart of hearts
you believe an attack on your person is imminent, then you
should attack first. A split second of indecision in the savage,
violent world of the 20th century can mean the difference between
life and death, survival and destruction. If that sounds like
exaggeration, come and stand on the night club door with me when
it kicks off and then tell me I'm wrong. Any man in front of me who
gives out threatening vibes is in grave danger of being 'caned.'

The theory that I spout is not mine alone. All the great
commanders of world wars, civil wars or any war for that matter
will tell you - shoot first and don't wait to be shot at. Admiral
Woodward of Falklands war fame sank the Belgrano because he
deemed it threatening. Had he waited for the Belgrano to attack,
he and his crew would very likely not be here now.

Coventry is a violent city, and seems at times in grave danger of
industrial emaciation, but it's the city of my birth and I love it. The
violence here, and everywhere else for that matter, is carved into
the bark by a small minority of people burgeoning on discipline-
less schools and a judicial system that is laughable in its tolerance
for such people. Coventry's inhabitants are in the main lovely,
lovely people who tolerate the assiduous few because they have no
option, and deserve not the stigma 'sent to Coventry'. I employ
violence only against violence or its potential, to protect the
majority. If I and my kind do not stand on the doors of the pubs
and clubs in the city many innocent people would be hurt and
lawlessness would prevail.

You may also deem some of my doings scandalous and
barbaric and my views extreme, but in a free society they are my
choices and views, and I hope you can respect that. If I lived in a

friendlier environment where violence did not issue itself so liberally from the sore on the face of humanity's etiolated complexion, and life was not such a theatre of combat, I could safely commission the use of guile as opposed to force.

These days I still work the doors of Coventry, but only for financial reasons. As soon as my purse allows it I will resign my post and hang up my dicky bow, as it were. Why? Because my reason for working the door was never financial gain, and now that I have learned what I set out to learn I find myself bound to this dangerous trade by the icing on the cake, money. I live in a lovely house with my beautiful Sharon who treats me like porcelain and has shown me a kaleidoscope of happiness that I never thought existed. This, though, could all be lost pitilessly quickly with my liberty or my life should I kill or be killed in the line of duty. I am at present working on the comfortable Devon door and am privileged to be a part of the best 'door' in Coventry, under the head doormanship of Seymore, who is a gentleman and my ideal of a doorman.

I find myself often questioning and deeply examining the theories and tactics of violence that I have stood by for so long, and asking myself if there is a more affable alternative to counter violence. But no matter which way I look at it I come to the same unfortunate conclusion: with these people in this environment anything less would be ineffective and would put my safety and that of the people I protect in jeopardy.

In retrospect, I believe that I did it right. I have matriculated from the school of bestiality with honours. Adversity, though, has taught me that amity is indeed something to be cherished and that life is, in fact, beautiful. Violence and violent people are just the thorn that you get on every rose. The presence of the thorn should not stifle the sweet smell that the rose emits.

When I started working on the door I was a thin, scared young man, as nervous on my first door as a new climber facing a precipice. Life was my playground bully and I wanted to stop the bullying so that I could lead a happier, braver life. Karate gave me the moral fibre to approach the challenge, facing and handling it gave me backbone. I have now gone full circle. I am again that affable, gentle man, but with all my fears brought to heal I no longer allow life to bully me and I have instituted in my mind an iron discipline that crushes negativity flatter than a shadow.

I thank God for giving me the courage to face my demons and banish them forever. I hope this book has taught you how to do the same.

Other books and videos by Geoff Thompson

Bouncer   *The Geoff Thompson Story Part Two*
On the Door   *The Geoff Thompson Story Part Three*
Small Wars
The Pavement Arena
Real Grappling
Real Punching
Real Kicking
Real Head, Knees & Elbows
Dead Or Alive   *– Self-protection*
3 Second Fighter – The Sniper Option
Weight Training – For the Martial Artist
Animal Day   – Pressure Testing the Martial Arts
Fear   – The Friend of Exceptional People: techniques in controlling fear
Blue Blood on the Mat by Athol Oakley, Foreword by Geoff Thompson
Give Him To The Angels – *The Story Of Harry Greb* by James R Fair

The Ground Fighting Series: Vol. One   – Pins, the Bedrock
(books and videos)   Vol. Two   – Escapes
                                    Vol. Three   – Chokes and Strangles
                                    Vol. Four   – Arm Bars and Joint Locks
                                    Vol. Five   – Fighting From Your Back
                                    Vol. Six   – Fighting From Neutral Knees

Videos:
Lessons with Geoff Thompson
Animal Day   – Pressure Testing the Martial Arts
Animal Day Part Two   – The Fights
Three Second Fighter   – The Sniper Option
Throws and Take-Downs Vols. 1-6
Real Punching Vols. 1-3
The Fence

Advanced Ground Fighting Vols. 1-3
(videos)
Pavement Arena Part 1
Pavement Arena Part 2   – The Protection Pyramid
Pavement Arena Part 3   – Grappling, The Last Resort
Pavement Arena Part 4   – Fit To Fight